BIZARRE
Bible Stories

BIZARRE
Bible Stories
Flying Pigs, Walking Bones,
and 24 Other Things That Really Happened

Dan Cooley
Illustrated by Garry Colby

Baker Books
A Division of Baker Book House Co
Grand Rapids, Michigan 49516

Published by Baker Books
a division of Baker Book House Company
P.O. Box 6287, Grand Rapids, MI 49516-6287
www.bakerbooks.com

Printed in the United States of America

Library of Congress Cataloging-in-Publication Data
Cooley, Dan, 1957–
     Bizarre Bible stories : flying pigs, walking bones, and 24 other things that really happened /
Dan Cooley.
          p.   cm.
     Includes bibliographical references (p.   ) and index.
     ISBN 0-8010-4520-7 (cloth)
     1. Bible stories. [1. Bible stories.] I. Title.
BS547.3.C66 2004
220.9′505—dc22   2003017273

Contents

Parent to Parent

My old seminary prof said, "It's a sin to make the Bible boring." My four children agree. If you're looking for a predictable children's Bible story book, don't buy this one. There are no stories about Jonah and the great fish in here. If you're expecting a story about David and Goliath, you'll be disappointed. This book even does the unthinkable in a children's devotional: It skips Noah and the flood completely! Based on limitless research into the lives of my children, I've concluded that a new story beats a rerun every time. The excitement of the Bible is its unpredictability. You never know what the omniscient God is going to do—unless, of course, you've heard the story before. Find your kids, their pajamas, and a few minutes of time. I promise they (and you) won't be bored. I've put four tips for you in each chapter. Here's how they work:

Tip #1—Scripture Passage

You can use the Scripture in a few ways. If you're in a hurry, you can simply ignore it. Admit it; sometimes you will! That's okay; I wrote the stories so you can dive right in and tell them without any preparation. If you have time to read the passage over before telling the story, you're type "A." That's terrific, and I'll ignore the guilt I feel for being less driven. However, what will probably happen is you'll be reading the story to your children and be silently thinking (with them), "No way that's in the Bible!" Then, not wanting to teach your kids what isn't true, you can read the story in the Bible after telling it to your kids. Your conscience will feel better knowing it's a true Bible story!

I've provided Scripture verses at the end of each chapter to help your children understand how the story relates to them. You could pick one verse to memorize or just read all the verses at the end. Some of the passages are terrific to use as a bedtime prayer. Or you can skip them altogether. They're parallel passages that fit with the "So What?" of the story, described in "Tip #2."

Tip #2—So What?

The beginning of each chapter has a "so what" explanation of why we're telling this Bible story to our children. It's the application of the story. Sometimes it's obvious, other times not. More than once I thought, "Now I know why no one told me these stories. They're impossible to understand! Why did God put them in here anyway?" Of course, finding the answer to that question is what adds excitement to the Bible and to the stories. I've included an index at the end of the book so you can find stories based on specific passages of Scripture or on the "so what" application topics. That way you can skip to a specific topic if you like. The stories are arranged according to the biblical time line, so some later stories may refer to previous ones. But, you're smart—you're a parent after all—and you can deal with that.

Tip #3—For Parents: [Anything in brackets]

There are a few difficulties in telling Bible stories to children. One is the "R" rating many of the stories would have in a movie version:

David walking back with a bleeding head the size of a basketball tucked under his arm; people screaming and clawing to climb into the ark as the rain continues to fall. You can even read about family trees that have no branches. Here's what I did. If you tell the story as written, your children should understand it with a "G" rating. In brackets, I've included more information about the story. It might be background information, gory details, resources, even a little parental humor. Include what you think your kids should know and skip the rest.

Tip #4—Questions

Each story contains a number of questions for your kids to answer. On those nights when you worked late, the kids are hyperactive, and you need them in bed pronto to preserve your sanity, skip the questions. On the other hand, when you have a little extra time or when the kids can sleep in the next day, ask *all* the questions. Your kids will love them, and you will be shocked at some of their answers. An interactive, unpredictable Bible story is what we're after, and the questions are key. Just stay sane, okay?

Talking Animals

Scripture Passage: Numbers 22

So What? God knows what you're thinking!

For Parents: [Anything in brackets]

> Have you ever sneezed and had someone say, "Bless you"?
> What do people mean by that? Does it give you a blessing?
> What would happen if someone said, "Curse you"? What would
> that mean? What would that do?

Some people believe strongly in blessing and cursing things. This is especially true for those who worship the earth, or Satan, or other false gods. When they bless things or people, sometimes it seems good things happen to them. When they curse things or people, it seems bad things happen to them.

Years ago, the king of Moab wanted to curse the Jewish people because he was afraid they were going to attack his country. He hired

11

a man named Balaam to do the cursing. It seemed that whenever Balaam cursed or blessed people, he got results. He was getting rich just going around cursing or blessing other people for hire. That wasn't a bad job! It paid well, and everyone seemed to like him.

Maybe you would go to Balaam and say, "Hey, I don't like my little brother. Can you put a curse on him—nothing too bad—for this weekend?" "Sure," Balaam might say, "for ten bucks." So you would pay him, and he would do it. On the other hand, maybe you would pay him to bless your next soccer game or your math test.

Balaam's blessings and curses really came true. Sometimes this may have been just luck, but other times it was more than luck. He lived on the shores of a big river called the Euphrates. Scientists have been able to dig up the old towns on the bank of the Euphrates from when Balaam lived. They found a lot of things that were used to worship demons. They're similar to things used today for voodoo, witchcraft, and New Age and occult religions. Balaam believed in all kinds of gods. He was successful in bringing blessings and curses because the demons of these gods were doing things for him. He was a very dangerous man, and he was making a lot of money.

How many true gods are there? How do you talk to God? Can you order him to do things for you?

Balak, the evil king of Moab, wanted to curse the Jewish people. So he said, "Balaam! Hey, Balaam! I'll pay you big bucks to call curses down on Israel." Balaam liked the sound of that. Big bucks were what he liked.

The way Balaam called down blessings or curses on people was to talk to their false god. Behind every false god is a demon. He would talk to the demon, and the demon would do things for him. "No problem," thought Balaam. "I'll just talk to the god/demon of these Jewish people, and he will curse them for me. And I'll make big bucks on it." However, when he spoke to this God, things were different. This wasn't a fake god; this was the REAL God. This God didn't take orders—this God *gave* orders. God ordered Balaam not to curse the Jews; he could bless them but not curse them.

Do you like to go on trips? Where is your favorite place to go? Has your car ever broken down on a long trip? What happened?

God told Balaam he could go to see the evil king, but he couldn't curse the Jews. Balaam packed up and got ready to go. He thought to himself, "The king will pay me lots of gold. I'll be rich if I call curses down on Israel. So I won't do what the God of the Israelites wants me to do. Their God will think I'm going to bless the Jews. But when I show up, I'll call curses down on them. I'll get rich. Their God can't stop me because he doesn't know what I am going to do! I'll sure surprise him!"

Balaam didn't tell anybody what he was thinking. It isn't even written down in this part of the Bible. [It's alluded to later in 2 Peter 2:15–16, and Jude 11.] However, we know what he was thinking because of what happened next.

Balaam saddled his donkey and started to ride out to meet the evil king, the king of Moab. He was probably whistling his favorite song to himself, thinking of how he was going to spend all that money. Suddenly, his donkey bolted off the path, taking Balaam with him. Smack! Balaam hit her on the side of the head. "Stupid donkey!" he yelled. "Stay on the lousy path!"

A little later the path became narrower, with a wall on both sides. Balaam was again lost in thought, spending the money he didn't yet have. Whack! The donkey smashed Balaam's foot against one of the walls! She continued to walk ahead. Thump! Balaam hit her harder. "You idiot," he yelled. "Keep it up, and you'll be my supper meat!"

The walls on the sides of the path got even closer together. The donkey and Balaam couldn't fit through. So the donkey stopped. Balaam wanted her to go on, but she wouldn't. Then she laid down! There Balaam was, sitting on top of a donkey that was lying on the ground between two walls. "That's it," said Balaam. "You're supper now!" He took his staff—a big stick—and began to beat her.

What animals do you have? Have you ever talked to them? Do they answer? [If they answer "Yes," you have your parental work cut out for you!]

About this time, Jesus gave the bruised donkey the ability to speak. The donkey asked Balaam, "What have I done to deserve you beating me three times today?" What would you do if your animals started talking to you? I bet you wouldn't do what Balaam did.

Balaam started talking back to her as if it was normal! Balaam answered the donkey, "You made a fool of me, donkey! If I had a sword in my hand, I'd kill you right now!"

Why wasn't Balaam surprised that his donkey was talking? Can you think of another time in the Bible when an animal spoke? It's in the very beginning.

Satan once talked to Eve through a snake. That's when Eve was tempted to eat the forbidden fruit in the Garden of Eden. In a story in the New Testament, demons enter pigs. That's a story for later in this book. Okay, we know that demons can enter animals if God lets them. We know that Satan spoke through a snake. We know that demons entered pigs. We know that Balaam talked with demons before. It's possible Balaam talked with demons in animals before.

Was there a demon in the donkey on this day? No, it was just the donkey in the donkey! So the donkey said back to Balaam, "Aren't I your own donkey and haven't you ridden me often? Have I ever acted like this before?" Balaam answered, "Um . . . no. In fact, until today you've been a fine donkey."

Then the Lord opened Balaam's eyes. He saw the angel of the Lord standing in the road with his sword drawn! [This is probably Jesus. It seems that O.T. references to the angel of the Lord are references to God himself. The story of Gideon in Judges 6 is an example of "the angel of the LORD" later being referred to as "The LORD."] Now Balaam knew why his donkey kept stopping. Quickly Balaam bowed low with his face in the dirt. The angel of the Lord asked Balaam, "Why have you beaten your donkey three times? I have come here to block your way because you are stubbornly resisting me. It's a good thing you had that donkey with you. If you didn't, you would be dead by now. I would have killed you, but I wanted to spare the donkey, and I couldn't hit you without injuring her!"

Wow, imagine God telling you that your pet is worth more to him than you are! Balaam learned a hard lesson. He learned that God knows your thoughts, even when you haven't told them to any other person. When God says to give him your heart, he means to give him even your thoughts. You may as well let God in on all your thoughts and plans; he knows them anyway. That way you will always be worth much more to him than your pet, whether it is a talking pet or not!

When Balaam left that place, his donkey took him straight to the evil king. There God blessed the Israelites through Balaam. The evil king wanted curses, but God brought blessings. When you let God in on your plans, blessing is the result!

Remember: You've Got His Word on It

How can I know all the sins lurking in my heart? Cleanse me from these hidden faults. Psalm 19:12

I have not kept this good news hidden in my heart; I have talked about your faithfulness and saving power. I have told everyone in the great assembly of your unfailing love and faithfulness. Psalm 40:10

How we praise God, the Father of our Lord Jesus Christ, who has blessed us with every spiritual blessing in the heavenly realms because we belong to Christ. Ephesians 1:3

And so it is: All who put their faith in Christ share the same blessing Abraham received because of his faith. . . . Through the work of Christ Jesus, God has blessed the Gentiles with the same blessing he promised to Abraham, and we Christians receive the promised Holy Spirit through faith. . . . So don't get tired of doing what is good. Don't get discouraged and give up, for we will reap a harvest of blessing at the appropriate time. Galatians 3:9, 14; 6:9

I have hidden your word in my heart, that I might not sin against you. Psalm 119:11

2

Outnumbered by One Bad Guy

Scripture Passage: Joshua 7

So What? Hidden sin hurts others!

For Parents: [Anything in brackets]

Do you know the story of Joshua and the battle of Jericho? [Or *Josh and the Big Wall* for all our Veggie-Tales fans.] Can you tell it to me?

Joshua and his army won the battle of Jericho. Before that battle, God commanded them not to take anything in the city for themselves. When the walls fell down they were supposed to go right through the city. What they did take, like gold and silver, they were to save and put aside for when they made a temple for God.

If you had all the money in the world, what would you want to buy?

Achan was walking through Jericho after the walls fell down. He looked in an empty house and saw a beautiful robe and thousands of dollars in gold and silver. Achan needed the money, and he had always wanted a robe just like the one he saw. It was even his size! So he took the robe and the money and hid them under his tent. No one knew Achan had stolen. No one saw him take the stuff or bury it. He hid his sin completely, and did it when he was alone, so no one could get hurt, right?

Have you ever had something terrible happen that you didn't understand? What was it? Why do you think God allowed it to happen?

God wanted Joshua to attack another city after Jericho. It was a little city called Ai.

Joshua sent an army of three thousand men to battle Ai. They got ready. They polished their shields. They sharpened their swords. They exercised. They prayed. They weren't too worried, because Ai was a small, wimpy city. It wasn't a big city with huge walls like Jericho. "This will be no problem," the men probably thought. Then they attacked Ai. All three thousand of them fought against the little city. Their shields were shiny. Their swords were sharp. They were in shape. They had even prayed the night before. But when they went into battle against the wimpy city, they lost. They lost big.

The army of Ai killed thirty-six of the men from Joshua's army. Thirty-six boys no longer had dads. Thirty-six wives no longer had husbands. Thirty-six moms and dads no longer had their boys. Thirty-six brothers were gone forever.

Joshua felt horrible. He bowed down. He cried. He prayed. He wouldn't eat. He could hardly sleep. He kept asking God, "Why did this happen? How could this happen? I don't understand! We came all the way from Egypt. We've waited all this time to go into the Promised Land. We won the battle of Jericho. Now we've lost the war of Ai. What are we going to do? We have thirty-six men to bury. This is awful!"

What is sin? [Disobeying God, missing the target of living like he wants us to.] Sin often hurts other people. Can you think of a time when someone's sin hurt you? [Being called names, having something stolen, etc.] Can you think of a time when you have hurt others?

You know what God said when Joshua was down on the ground praying? God said, "Stand up!" He then told Joshua someone had sinned by stealing in Jericho. God had told the Israelites not to take anything out of Jericho, but someone did. God led Joshua to Achan.

Because of Achan's hidden sin, thirty-six people died. Hidden sin hurts those around us. If Achan had turned his behavior around and admitted—or confessed—his sin, he would have been forgiven. God always forgives those who confess their sins. However, Achan hid his sin instead. It wasn't until Joshua caught Achan and confronted him with his sin that Achan admitted he had stolen. That's not confessing your sin; that's just being caught.

Where did Achan put the stuff he stole? He put it in the dark; he hid it under his tent. What he didn't realize is God can see in the dark! God is light, and he saw that sin as if it was sitting on the dining room table.

Because of his sin, Achan died the same day Joshua caught him. The Bible says, "You may be sure that your sin will find you out . . . the wages of sin is death" (Num. 32:23; Rom. 6:23). Achan tried to hide his sin, and he died for it. If we believe in Jesus and confess our sins to him, he will wash them away. He can do that because he already died for our sin in our place. Only we cannot try to hide it. We must admit [confess] our sin to him. The rest of Romans 6:23 says, "the free gift of God is eternal life through Jesus Christ our Lord."

Achan tried to take care of his sin by hiding it. That never works. It only hurts others and us. God says to take care of our sin by admitting it! Give it to Jesus, and his light will wash it away.

Joshua and his army went back to Ai. This time they won the war! The first time they had been outnumbered by the sin of one bad guy. He wasn't bad because he sinned [we've all done that]; he was bad because he covered it rather than admitting it.

Remember: You've Got His Word on It

Believe on the Lord Jesus and you will be saved. Acts 16:31

God saved you by his special favor when you believed. And you can't take credit for this; it is a gift from God. Salvation is not a reward for the good things we have done, so none of us can boast about it. Ephesians 2:8–9

He saved us, not because of the good things we did, but because of his mercy. He washed away our sins and gave us a new life through the Holy Spirit. Titus 3:5

3

Race to Jail

Scripture Passage: Joshua 20–21

So What? Jesus is our refuge!

For Parents: [Anything in brackets]

In the Bible there are places called "cities of refuge." Do you know what the word *refuge* means? [It means "a place of safety."] Knowing that, what do you think the cities of refuge were?

The cities of refuge were places of safety. After the Israelites entered the Promised Land with Joshua, they needed to get things organized. They needed a fire department, doctors, hospitals, police officers, and jails. This was a lot to do, and Joshua didn't have much time to do it.

So, instead of having a police department and jails, God had Joshua set up cities of refuge.

What do you think would happen in our town if all the police left? What might happen if all the jails closed down and the prisoners escaped?

The Bible says we are all sinners. That means all of us have disobeyed God. Sometimes when people sin, when they disobey God, they are disobeying the government as well. That makes them criminals. Our governments punish criminals in order for the rest of us to be safe. Our city wouldn't be safe if there were no police department. The police help keep us safe by catching people who are doing evil things to others. With the criminals in jail, the rest of us are safe.

Who would keep us safe if there were no police? We would have to keep each other safe. That's how they did things in Joshua's time. If someone snuck into your house and stole all your favorite toys, you would have to find the criminal. You would get your friends together, catch the person, and take him or her to court. There the elders and judges of the city would decide what they should do with the accused criminal. You and your friends would be your own police department!

Being your own police department could be a dangerous way to live. This was especially true when someone died. Sometimes people died because they were murdered. Other times people died because an animal killed them or they were in a farming accident. If someone in your family was murdered, it would be up to your family to find the murderer. You would again need to get all your friends together and hunt down the person you believed to be the murderer. Then, according to the law, it was okay for you to—now get this; you won't believe it—it was okay for you to kill the murderer! Wow, when you were your own police, you really had a lot of power! You were like the police, the judge, and the jury all at once!

[Western movies illustrate how the Old Testament system worked. The bank robbers would ride out of town, and the sheriff would get the "posse" together. The posse protecting its town is similar to the O.T. system of the larger family and their friends protecting their own.]

What do you think could go wrong if you were your own police department? If you broke your mother's favorite lamp by accident, what might happen to you? If you smashed that same lamp on purpose, what might happen to you? Why is there a difference?

One problem with being your own police department is that you can make mistakes! Wouldn't it be awful if you killed someone for being a murderer and he was the wrong person? Then someone would hunt you down and kill you for killing the wrong person. What a mess!

Another problem was accidental killings. What would happen if someone died in a farming accident, but the family thought you killed the person on purpose? The law said they could hunt you down and kill you, because you killed their family member. It was a farming accident—you didn't want to kill anybody. But they don't know that, and now they're coming for you! It isn't an easy world without police!

It was because of these possible errors that God had Joshua build cities of refuge. The purpose of the cities was to give you a safe place to run to if a family was chasing you. Let's pretend you and a friend were putting hay up in a barn. You drop your pitchfork and it hits your friend down below! You feel terrible. You run down the steps and see that your friend has already died. Just then, his brother comes running up and yells, "You killed him; you killed him! I'm going to get my family; we're going to kill you!" What could you do? You could run to a city of refuge.

Joshua built six of these cities. He built them up high on hills so the people could see them from far away. He put pastors [O.T. Levites who had rotating jobs in the Tabernacle] in charge of them. He had wide roads made to each of the cities of refuge. The Levites made certain the roads were always in the best shape, so people could travel fast on them. They were wide, flat, and smooth, and went straight up the hills to the cities. These were the best, widest, smoothest roads in all Israel. At every turn in the road, there was a sign that said "Refuge" with an arrow pointing the way to run, so the person running would not get lost. Joshua made every attempt to make sure that the person could get to the city in safety.

> **What do you think it would be like to live in one of the cities of refuge? What do you think it would be like to go to jail?**

Once you made it to the city, you could run inside and be safe. Yes! But the danger wasn't over yet. Guilty murderers would run to the cities of refuge as well. The cities of refuge had judges who would hold a trial. The judge would have to hear what really happened (Num. 35:12, 24).

If it was determined that you were guilty of murder, the judge would kick you out of the city of refuge! There wouldn't be a safe place for you anywhere in the entire country. The family of the one you murdered would continue to look for you. You would never be safe.

If you had killed someone by accident, then you could stay in the city. You were safe, but you were in a kind of jail. If you left the city, then the family of the one you murdered could kill you. Only in the city of refuge would you be safe. Like in our story of accidentally killing someone on the farm with the pitchfork, you would not be guilty of murder. But you would be guilty of being careless, and you would have to live in the city of refuge to be safe. There was protection inside the city but not outside the city (Num. 35:26–27).

The city of refuge was a little like jail, because you couldn't leave. However, it was nicer than going to jail. It was a safe place. Pastors [Levites], not prison guards, were in charge, and they ran things well. It wasn't a place of punishment. You could have your own place to live and raise your own food. Visitors could come to see you and spend time with you. It was a great place to live, safe and secure, until your time in the city was up. But how long would you have to stay?

You would have to stay in the city of refuge until the high priest died. Maybe the high priest was very young and healthy, and you would have to stay there for thirty years or more. Ugh! But it was also possible that the high priest was extremely sick when you entered, and he died soon afterward. In that case, you might only have to stay for a week. It didn't matter when you came in, everyone in the cities of refuge would leave together when the high priest died. The day after the high priest died, all the cities would be empty, except for the pastors [Levites] who worked and lived there. Wow, it would be a ghost town!

God had Joshua create the cities of refuge to make a safe place for people who did wrong accidentally. If they did wrong on purpose, they wouldn't be able to stay in the city. If it was an accident, the city was a safe place for them.

Jesus is a safe place for all who have

done wrong and are sorry for it. The road to Jesus is always wide, flat, and smooth, and it goes straight up to his home—heaven. Whenever we pray, he hears us. If we know Jesus and have done wrong, we need to run to him. He is our refuge. Jesus paid the price for our sin; he took our punishment so we don't have to pay it ourselves. Our judge, God the Father, will find us not guilty, because Jesus paid the punishment for our sin. Prayer never breaks down. The Bible has signs that tell us Jesus is our refuge, so we never have to be lost. Follow the signs to Jesus!

Remember: You've Got His Word on It

This I declare of the LORD: He alone is my refuge, my place of safety; he is my God, and I am trusting him. Psalm 91:2

But to the poor, O LORD, you are a refuge from the storm. To the needy in distress, you are a shelter from the rain and the heat. Isaiah 25:4

God cannot lie when he takes an oath or makes a promise. These two things can never be changed. Those of us who have taken refuge in him hold on to the confidence we have been given. Hebrews 6:18 GOD'S WORD

A highway will be there, a roadway. It will be called the Holy Road. Sinners won't travel on it. It will be for those who walk on it. Godless fools won't wander {onto it}. Isaiah 35:8 GOD'S WORD

Jesus answered him, "I am the way, the truth, and the life. No one goes to the Father except through me." John 14:6 GOD'S WORD

4

When Women Rule

Scripture Passage: Judges 4–5

So What? Jesus never leaves you alone!

For Parents: [Anything in brackets]

Do you remember what the cities of refuge were? [They were cities you could run to if you accidentally killed someone. No one could harm you once you were in the city. After you arrived in the city, there would be a trial. If the judges decided the killing was an accident, you could remain in the city in safety.]

In the Book of Judges, chapters four and five, the Bible tells us the Israelites were sinning again. They had forgotten God. As a result, God let Jabin, the king of Canaan, rule over the Israelites. Jabin was a wicked king with nine hundred iron chariots. Do you know what a chariot is? [You can describe it as a cart looking a little like Santa's sleigh but with wheels instead of skis on the bottom. One or two pairs of horses would race the iron chariots into battle, where the person in the cart could shoot the enemy with his bow.] Having nine hundred chariots at that time would be like having nine hundred tanks today. Jabin had an extremely powerful army!

This big army of chariots made King Jabin proud, and he was cruel to the Israelites for twenty years. He appointed a commander named Sisera, who was the cruelest of them all. The people in Israel began to wonder why God was letting this happen to them. It took twenty years before they realized they were being treated cruelly because they had forgotten God. God allowed this to happen to bring them back to him. Jabin, Sisera, and their warriors had power only because God allowed them to have power. When the Israelites realized this, they began to pray. They told God they were sorry for their sins, and asked him to forgive them for how they had been living. Then they asked God to take away Sisera and his evil army of chariots. And God answered.

> If some bullies were coming after you, who would you want to show up to protect you? Why did you choose that person? How would you like a woman named "Honeybee" to come to protect you?

Deborah is a Hebrew name. In English, it means "Honeybee." Honeybee was a prophet, a judge, and a leader in Israel. People went to her to settle arguments. They respected her because she listened to God and did what he said.

When the people prayed to God to protect them from Sisera and his nine hundred chariots, God talked to Honeybee. Honeybee sent for a man named Barak. She told Barak, "I want you to get an army together to meet Sisera in battle at Mount Tabor." Honeybee probably knew that no one would follow a woman named Honeybee to battle, so she needed Barak's help. Honeybee was smart. Mount

Tabor is thirteen hundred feet high. The chariots couldn't run up and down a mountain. The trees, rocks, riverbeds, and steep mountainside would stop the chariots. It would be a little like trying to drive your family minivan at an Olympic skateboard competition. It just wouldn't work!

Barak was the general of the army. But he was afraid. Nine hundred chariots with eighteen hundred horses running after you could put fear in any man. He knew if God was really with him, he would win the war. But how would he know God was with him? He decided he would trust Honeybee, but he was chicken to go without her. So, Barak said, "I'll go if you'll go; but, Honeybee, if you don't go with me, I won't go!" Who was braver, Barak or Honeybee? Honeybee was! Wow, women can rule!

"Okay," said Honeybee, "I'll go with you. However, because you were chicken to follow God by yourself, the honor won't be yours. The honor will go to a woman who is not chicken to trust God. God will let a woman win the war and be the hero." Barak probably thought the hero would be Honeybee, but he was wrong!

Who is your favorite make-believe hero? Maybe it's Superman, Underdog [okay, that dates me], or Larry-Boy. Who is your real-life hero? Why is that person a hero to you?

Barak called his warriors together. Sisera heard about it and went with his nine hundred chariots to kill Barak and his army. Honeybee and Barak and his army ran to Mount Tabor. Sisera and all his chariots went to Mount Tabor to meet them.

When Honeybee saw the chariots, she said to Barak, "Hurry up! Let's go! Today God is going to wipe out those chariots. God's answering our prayers!"

So Barak went to fight Sisera and his chariot army and it was a total blowout. The Israelites wasted them. The mountain was so rough Sisera's men had to get out of their chariots to fight. Sisera's whole army was defeated, but not Sisera. He decided he'd better run before someone saw him and killed him.

Sisera's only chance was to run to the closest city of refuge, so that's probably where he was headed. He needed to get to safety; he wanted to kill the Israelites, but he didn't want them to kill him! Sisera ran as far as he could, but he couldn't make it to the city in one day. Mount Tabor was too far away from the closest city of refuge. He needed to find a place to spend the night, but where could he go? Where could he be safe?

Sisera saw a city made of tents down in the valley. These were nomadic people; they lived in tents instead of houses so they could move around and raise their animals. They had many sheep and goats that had to keep moving to find pasture. These nomadic people didn't care for politics and war. They kept to themselves. The women would put up the tents and take care of the city while the men were out caring for the animals. "That's where I'll go," thought Sisera. "The men are probably off somewhere with the animals. The women can't hurt me. They will protect me, even if I am evil. I'll spend the night with them and then run to safety."

Jael lived in the tent city with her family. She was inside her tent when Sisera, the Canaanite general, ran up. Jael was home alone, but she knew she had to let him in. He could kill her in an instant. She invited him into her tent, covered him with a blanket, and gave him something to drink.

Jael knew who Sisera was. She knew he was the Canaanite general of the nine-hun-dred-chariot army. She knew he was at war with Israel. She knew she was hiding the most important man in the enemy's army. That night, with her husband gone watching the animals and Sisera asleep in her tent, she did what Barak didn't do. She did what Honeybee didn't do. She did what nobody should want to do but what had to be done. Jael killed Sisera while he was sleeping! [Depending on the age of your children, you can give them the full biblical story. She used a tent stake and nailed him to the ground through his forehead! Sisera went to bed and woke up dead.] For him it was a painless death. For the armies of Israel and Canaan, it was the end of the war. For Israel, it was the beginning of following God again.

> Why did God pick Honeybee to rule in Israel? What made Jael the hero? Why was Barak not a hero? How did he live differently from the two women?

On the day of the battle, women ruled. They ruled because they followed God when no one else did. Honeybee was ready to go to war against nine hundred chariots. Barak was also willing, but only if Honeybee went with him. He was afraid to go alone. He didn't trust God like Honeybee did. Jael trusted God when no one was with her. Her husband was gone, and she was alone with the evil general of the Canaanites. She could have let him stay in her tent overnight and leave the next day. No one would have said bad things about her. After all, what can one woman do against a general? However, Jael knew what she could and should do, and she did it. She followed God when she was all alone.

The hardest time to follow Jesus is when you feel alone. Others may want you to do what is wrong, and no one will support you. Still, you must follow Jesus. Sometimes it's easy to follow Jesus when you're with a group of Christian friends or family, but sometimes you feel alone. Remember, you can never be alone when you are following Christ; he is right there with you! And when you follow Jesus, you are his hero!

Remember: You've Got His Word on It

Do you think anyone is going to be able to drive a wedge between us and Christ's love for us? There is no way! Not trouble, not hard times, not hatred, not hunger, not homelessness, not bullying threats, not backstabbing, not even the worst sins listed in Scripture. . . . None of this fazes us because Jesus loves us. I'm absolutely convinced that nothing— nothing living or dead, angelic or demonic, today or tomorrow, high or low, thinkable or unthinkable—absolutely *nothing* can get between us and God's love because of the way that Jesus our Master has embraced us. Romans 8:35–39 MESSAGE

5

The God Who Worshipped God

Scripture Passage: 1 Samuel 5

So What? Only one God deserves our worship!

For Parents: [Anything in brackets]

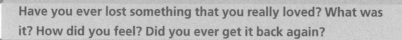

Have you ever lost something that you really loved? What was it? How did you feel? Did you ever get it back again?

During the time when Samuel was a prophet, God's people stopped following him. They were getting selfish and lazy and they forgot about God. This time the Israelites' sin caused the loss of their most important treasure. You see, by forgetting God and going their own way, God's people lost a battle with the Philistines. During the battle they lost, the Philistines took the Israelites' most important

33

treasure—"the Ark." That same Ark may still be on our planet, hidden somewhere. It would be wonderful to find.

Have you ever wondered what it might be like to live in heaven? Wouldn't it be great if someone went up there with a camera and brought you back the pictures? That's impossible, of course, but God wants us to know what his home is like, so he gave us another kind of picture. He had Moses build the Ark.

The Ark, which God told Moses to build, was a box about four feet long, two feet high, and two feet deep [use hands to illustrate the size, not much different than a toy box]. It was made of wood and covered with gold. The lid was made of solid gold and was called "the mercy seat." *Mercy* means "kindness" and "forgiveness." *Seat* means "place." On top of the gold lid were two large angels called cherubim. The Ark was a picture of Jesus' home, heaven. It's a place of kindness, forgiveness, and powerful angels. Inside the Ark Moses placed the Israelites' most special treasure—the Ten Commandments, which were written on two stones by God himself. Where do you keep your special treasures?

Now, the battle was lost, and the Ark was gone. The gold was gone. The gifts that were inside the Ark were gone.

What are some things people love more than God? What did people in Old Testament times worship besides God?

Many people in Old Testament times worshipped statues. It seems silly to us now, to worship something that we made, but that's what they did. Sometimes we still do this. We might worship our cars, toys, friends, or favorite sports teams. We worship whatever we love the most. If we sacrifice for an entire year to buy a toy, then give all our savings for that toy and put it on a shelf to look at every day, we've started worshipping the toy. That kind of worship is sinful. We must worship God and God alone.

The Philistines who took the Ark worshipped a statue named Dagon. They believed he was the most powerful god around. For almost 1,000 years, they had worshipped Dagon! After winning the battle, the Philistines took the Ark to the temple for Dagon. "O great Dagon," they probably said, "we praise you for winning the battle today. Here is a present for you. This Ark symbolizes the weak god we defeated today." What a statue would do with a gold box is beyond me, but the Philistines thought Dagon would like it.

How do you think the one true God felt now? His gift of the Ark was now in the temple of a false god!

The Philistines stole the Ark of God and gave it to a statue—a false god! But God, the only true God, wasn't surprised. He knew this would happen. It had to happen because his people had stopped following him. They needed to come back to him. God knew that losing the battle, the Ark, and the treasures would cause them to do just that. God always has a plan, and this one was going to be fun! He would show the Philistines who the true God really was.

The next day the Philistines came to Dagon's temple to worship. "Hey, where's Dagon? Who moved him?" the first one asked. "Over here!" someone screamed. "And look! He's down in the dirt worshipping the God of the Ark!"

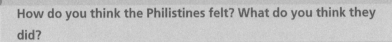

How do you think the Philistines felt? What do you think they did?

The Philistines were embarrassed. They quickly picked up their statue of Dagon and put him back in his place. "No way can Dagon bow down to the God of the Ark," they thought. "We won the battle, after all." So they put Dagon in his place, worshipped the old statue, and went home.

Early the next morning they came back to worship Dagon again. "No, it couldn't be, not again!" they screamed. Dagon was bowing down in the dirt in front of the Ark—again—only this time it was much worse. This time Dagon's head and hands were gone! They looked around and found that someone had cut the statue's head and hands off and left them lying by the door! Who could have done this? They realized the true God must have cut off the head and hands from the statue!

Now the Philistines knew the God of the Ark must be more powerful than Dagon. If the statue they believed in had to bow to the God of the Ark, then shouldn't they bow too? The God of the Ark broke their most powerful god, so he must be the most powerful God of all! They made sure that the Ark went back where it belonged.

What does worship mean? Who deserves our worship?

To worship means to bow down or to serve. We worship what we love the most. Philippians 2:10–11 says, "at the name of Jesus every knee should bow, in heaven and on earth and under the earth, and every tongue confess that Jesus Christ is Lord, to the glory of God the Father" (NIV). When we obey God, when we bow down and pray to him, we worship him. Let's do that now.

Remember: You've Got His Word on It

There is only one God worthy of worship. One of the clearest passages for those who might believe or teach otherwise is Isaiah 43:10–13:

"You have been chosen to know me, believe in me, and understand that I alone am God. There is no other God; there never has been and never will be. I am the LORD, and there is no other Savior. First I predicted your deliverance; I declared what I would do, and then I did it—I saved you. No foreign god has ever done this before. You are witnesses that I am the only God," says the LORD. "From eternity to eternity I am God. No one can oppose what I do. No one can reverse my actions."

6

How to Scare a Witch

Scripture Passage: 1 Samuel 28

So What? If you make rules, keep them!

For Parents: [Anything in brackets]

> Who is your best friend? Have you ever had a perfect day? What happened?

About three thousand years ago Samuel died. He was a great man who loved God; now he is living with God, and he's very glad to be there too. He has no more chores, a completely new world to explore, and dreams to come true. (It is like having your best day with your best friend and it never ends.) That's life for Samuel.

At the same time, back on earth, Saul is king. Being king should be great! Saul is rich and famous. He can buy whatever he wants. Life should be paradise for Saul, but it isn't. Saul is in the middle of a war, and he's losing. Right now, he's living in a tent instead of his castle, and he needs Samuel's advice quick. Samuel often gave Saul advice when he was alive. However, Samuel died. That's a bummer for Saul, because the war is going badly, and only Samuel can give Saul the advice he needs.

> Do you ask God for advice? Does he answer? God can give advice many ways. It may come through your parents, the Bible, circumstances, godly friends, or even an angel or God himself! [As for me, he usually answers just in time, which is much later than I would like.]

Why does Saul need Samuel? You would think that Saul could just ask God for advice. We do that. We read the Bible, we talk to God, and God hears us. Things didn't work that way for Saul. He had followed God when he was younger, but not anymore. Now Saul's life is majorly messed up. You name the sin, and he was probably guilty of it. Saul felt too guilty to talk to God. Samuel was dead, so Saul couldn't go to him for advice either. What could Saul do?

When Saul was younger, he made a good law that said there could be no witchcraft in his kingdom. One way to practice witchcraft is to contact people who have died. Saul decided that he would break his own law, find a witch, and contact the dead prophet Samuel through her!

Could a witch really contact dead people? Don't you hate it when people break their own rules? Can you remember a time when your parents did that? [Sorry.]

Can someone who has died come back to earth and talk to us? Except for rare exceptions, when God allows someone to be raised from the dead, the answer is NO. What witches do, sometimes, is to trick people. They can trick people two different ways. First, they may trick the people by talking like the dead person. Another possibility is that a demon may come and talk, sounding like the person who died. Either way it is something God tells his people not to be part of. Only God can bring people back from the dead. Anything else is a trick from a witch [sounding like the dead person] or a demon [also sounding like the dead person]. People cannot contact the dead, but Saul doesn't know that.

Well, Saul decides to go see a witch, against his own law. His friends find a witch close by. Nervously he hides his robes and crown. He puts on other clothes. He doesn't want anyone to know he is going out to break his own rule! He and his friends sneak out of their tents late at night. They step around sleeping soldiers in the battlefield. Finally they make it to town. Slowly, walking in the shadows, they find their way in the dark to the witch's house. She lets them in. They sit around a table lit with candles. The witch prepares to get in touch with her demon. God is watching. Saul is scared to death. His friends are wondering what they are doing there. Meanwhile Samuel is in paradise with God, having a wonderful time.

In the Bible God asks us to do things for him. What are some things that you can do for God?

The witch asks Saul, "What person do you want me to bring back from the dead?"

"Bring up Samuel."

It's hard to know exactly what happened next. We do know Samuel shows up, but we aren't told how he gets there. It might have been something like this . . .

The demon prepares to enter the room to trick Saul into believing he is Samuel. This will be easy. The demon had practiced Samuel's voice. He is ready. Suddenly huge powerful angels surround the demon. Their eyes look like fire. Their swords are drawn and ready to swing. One angel, larger than the rest, rushes at him. The demon cowers. The angel's sword flashes and swings to his neck, stopping when it touches his demonic skin. The fiery angel calmly says, "You won't be serving your witch tonight. Jesus has other plans!"

Meanwhile, Samuel is having another terrific day when God asks him to do something for him.

"What do you have in mind?" Samuel asks.

"Well, Samuel, Saul has got himself into a mess again. He's in the middle of a war that isn't going well. He wanted advice from you about the war so badly that he is breaking his own law. He has gone to see a witch to bring you back from the dead."

"Surely he knows better than that! A witch can't bring anyone back from the dead! The witch will trick him. What's wrong with Saul? He's breaking his own laws!"

"Listen closely, Samuel; I want you to play a trick on the witch who wants to trick Saul. I'll have a few angels keep her demon busy, while you pop in and tell Saul the truth."

Have you ever been super-surprised? What happened? Did you scream? Can you give me your loudest scream right now? [Depending on your children's lung capacity, you may want to have them scream into their pillow!]

When the witch saw Samuel, she screamed. "AAAHHHHH-GGGGG!!!!!!" She must have wondered, "What happened to my poor demon? How in the world did Samuel get here? Who in the universe has enough power to trick a witch? How come I'm scared? I'm the witch!"

The Bible doesn't say what happened to the witch or her demon. The Bible does say what happened to Saul. Samuel told Saul that because of his sin, he would lose the war and his life. He would have been wiser to keep his own rules!

Remember: You've Got His Word on It

If any among the people are unfaithful by consulting and following mediums or psychics, I will turn against them and cut them off from the community. So set yourselves apart to be holy, for I, the LORD, am your God. Keep all my laws and obey them, for I am the LORD, who makes you holy. Leviticus 20:6–8

You must be holy because I, the LORD, am holy. I have set you apart from all other people to be my very own. Leviticus 20:26

The person who rules righteously, who rules in the fear of God, he is like the light of the morning, like the sunrise bursting forth in a cloudless sky, like the refreshing rains that bring tender grass from the earth. 2 Samuel 23:3–4

When I learn your righteous laws, I will thank you by living as I should! I will obey your principles. Please don't give up on me! How can a young person stay pure? By obeying your word and following its rules. Psalm 119:7–9

7

Time for a Haircut

Scripture Passage: 2 Samuel 18

So What? Have mercy, and give others a second chance!

For Parents: [Anything in brackets]

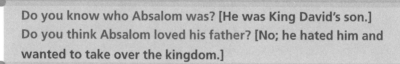

Do you know who Absalom was? [He was King David's son.]
Do you think Absalom loved his father? [No; he hated him and
wanted to take over the kingdom.]

Absalom wanted to be king instead of his father, King David. Absalom told lies about his father to get people to lose trust in his dad. Then he rounded up a lot of evil people who hated his father.

Absalom was ready for war. He got a big army together. He had David outnumbered. He was ready to defeat King David and become King Absalom.

King David would now have to fight his son Absalom. David could pick where the battle would be. Where should he go, to the open fields or the forest?

David decided to run as fast as he and his army could go. They ran to the forest. He did this because he knew he was outnumbered. The forest would give David's army some protection. There they could hide behind trees. They could also climb trees and see a possible ambush. Absalom's army wouldn't be able to fight as well on their horses and chariots with trees all around.

A large army with lots of horses and chariots would rather fight in the open plains. There the horses could run fast, and the chariot drivers could catch people on foot. Since Absalom was picking the fight and was chasing David, David could stop and fight wherever he wanted. David wisely picked the forest.

When David and his army made it to the forest, he made his battle plans. He divided his army into three groups and told his commanders something odd. Even though his son Absalom was coming to kill him, David did not want Absalom killed! King David still loved his son, in spite of all Absalom had done. David told his three commanders to be gentle with Absalom. David knew they needed to capture his son, but he didn't want Absalom killed. David remembered God had shown mercy to him when he had done wrong. Now his son Absalom was doing wrong and David wanted to show his son mercy, in the same way that God had shown David mercy.

The army marched into the field to fight Israel, but David's army brought Absalom's army into the forest of Ephraim. The battle was fierce and spread out over the entire forest.

Twenty thousand men died in that horrible battle. The Bible says the forest killed more people than the sword. How could that be? How can a forest kill people?

The chariots and horses were running into trees. Some horses probably fell into pits because they were going too fast to see them. Other horses broke their legs while galloping over the rough ground. Branches seemed to come from nowhere and knock riders off their horses. Absalom's army was having a rotten day.

Absalom himself was riding a mule instead of a horse. A mule is an animal that's half horse and half donkey. It's slower but stronger than a horse. A horse can carry one person, sometimes two. A mule can carry as much weight as three people or more; also, a mule is much more surefooted. [There are trails going down the Grand Canyon in Arizona. Horses can't go down those trails because they aren't sure-footed enough. Mules, however, go down those same trails all the time, as do people with a low IQ and/or no fear of heights.] Absalom was smart. He was on a mule so he could fight in the forest!

Suddenly, Absalom was in a bad spot. He saw the army of David coming toward him, and he was alone. Absalom whipped his mule around. He took off back through the forest in the other direction. An oak tree was coming up fast. The branches were low. He ducked but not low enough! The branches jammed around his head and caught in his long hair. His mule, which was running as fast as it could go, kept going. Absalom's sword and shield were on the mule. There Absalom was, hanging in the air a few feet off the ground. He couldn't wrench himself free from the tree. He was stuck, and David's soldiers were coming! How he wished he could cut his hair and get down!

David's men knew they were not to hurt Absalom, so they just left him up in the tree and stood around him! How humiliating! How Absalom's head must have hurt!

Some of David's men took off to tell the commanders that they had caught Absalom. How happy they were! This might end the battle, and no one else would have to die. One of David's soldiers found Joab, his commander. He told Joab what had happened. Certainly now Joab would blow his trumpet, call in the soldiers, and end the war. The other side would give up, knowing that the man they followed could never be king. He was now a prisoner. However, that's not what Joab did.

How would you feel if you were Absalom? What would you be thinking? What would you do if you were Joab? When is it hard for you to give someone a second chance?

Mercy means compassion, pity, to give someone a second chance. Absalom must have wondered why David's soldiers didn't kill him. King David had been merciful before, and Absalom hadn't understood why. Now Absalom was grateful for his father's mercy! But Commander Joab had no mercy.

Joab found Absalom hanging in the air just as the soldier had told him. Joab didn't obey King David; he killed Absalom. Then he blew his trumpet to call in the soldiers and end the war. He could have let Absalom live, but he didn't.

David must have been thrilled to hear the trumpet. He knew the battle was over. His army won! Then he found out his son was dead. Joab had messed up big time and suffered the consequences of his actions for the rest of his life. He lost command of the army to his cousin and was later killed for treason [supporting Adonijah over Solomon, as well as killing Abner and Amasa]. It was a sad end to the life of a great general, who should have listened to his king.

King David knew God had been merciful to him, and he needed to show mercy to others. God has given all of us second chances, and we need to do the same. Isn't it great to know God is like King

David, not like Joab? He loves you, in spite of anything bad you may have done. He is the God of second chances!

Remember: You've Got His Word on It

Never let loyalty and kindness get away from you! Wear them like a necklace; write them deep within your heart. Then you will find favor with both God and people, and you will gain a good reputation. Proverbs 3:3–4

Your own soul is nourished when you are kind, but you destroy yourself when you are cruel. Proverbs 11:17

Whoever pursues godliness and unfailing love will find life, godliness, and honor. Proverbs 21:21

O people, the LORD has already told you what is good, and this is what he requires: to do what is right, to love mercy, and to walk humbly with your God. Micah 6:8

God blesses those who are merciful, for they will be shown mercy. Matthew 5:7

You must be compassionate, just as your Father is compassionate. Luke 6:36

Since God chose you to be the holy people whom he loves, you must clothe yourselves with tenderhearted mercy, kindness, humility, gentleness, and patience. Colossians 3:12

8

The World's
Most Expensive Water

Scripture Passage: 2 Samuel 23

So What? Friendship is worth the risk!

For Parents: [Anything in brackets]

> Who is your best friend? What have your friends done for you?
> What have you done for them?

Many people think David was the greatest king in the history of Israel. He was powerful. He was kind. He wrote most of the Book of Psalms. He loved God, and God loved him.

David was also a strong warrior. He had to defend his country of Israel against many evil armies. The first time David had to fight in battle was against a giant named Goliath. You remember that story!

There were thousands of men in David's army; the Bible gives a list of thirty of his greatest fighters and friends. But there were three friends who were even more important and fiercer than the thirty. These were David's mightiest men.

What do you enjoy doing with your friends? What do you do to help your friends that isn't fun? [Clean your room or theirs; help with chores or schoolwork.] What do you think David's friends did with him?

David spent a lot of his time fighting. His country was at war. It's not that David liked to fight, but he had no choice if Israel was to remain free to worship God. Satan used people like Goliath to attack Israel. He wanted to make them slaves and to keep them from worshipping God. David and his friends spent a lot of time fighting together. They had to protect each other from swords and arrows coming to kill them. So, what do you think David's three friends, his mightiest men, were mighty in? Right, they were strong in battle.

The first (and probably the greatest) of the Three was Jashobeam. David called him "Sharp Spear." [Some versions of the Bible give the Hebrew transliteration in 2 Samuel 23:8. The meaning of the Hebrew word is "Sharp Spear." Either his parents had a great guess what his life would turn out like, or it was a nickname.] He probably earned this name in a battle he had to fight. In that one battle, he killed eight hundred enemy soldiers with his spear. I don't know how he did it, but he did. This is one guy you'd like on your side in a fight!

David's second mighty man was Eleazar, which means "God is my Helper." In one battle, Israel was badly outnumbered. The entire army ran away. That is, everybody except David and Eleazar. He and David stood their ground, and the entire Philistine army came against them. Back to back, they fought and won! Eleazar had been holding his sword so tight, for so long, he couldn't let go when it was over!

It was as if his hand had frozen to the sword hilt! The Israelite army didn't come back until the battle was over. They were certain David and Eleazar couldn't win. You know that David and Eleazar became close friends that day!

Shammah was the last of David's three mighty men. There was a battle where the Philistines attacked the Israelite army in a field. The Israelites ran, but Shammah stayed. He knew God would want the field defended. He took his stand in the middle of the field; he defended it, and God brought a great victory that day.

God brought all these victories, but he chose to bring the victories through three men who trusted him. That's what made these men special, and that's what made them close friends of David.

Have you ever been super thirsty? Your lips feel dry and cracked, your mouth starts to pucker, and your throat is sandy. What is your favorite thing to drink when you feel like that?

David was at war with the Philistines. Things looked bad. He and his men were hiding in mountain caves outside Bethlehem. The Philistines had already taken over the town of Bethlehem. Now they were looking for David and his army.

David and his men were hungry and super thirsty. They were stuck in the caves with nothing to eat or drink. Down in Bethlehem, the Philistines had all the food and drink they wanted. They even had water from the wells in Bethlehem. That was some of the best tasting water anywhere. David was thinking how unfair that seemed. He said, "Man, I can't believe we are stuck up here dying of thirst, and they have the wells of Bethlehem! I sure wish I had some of that clear, cold, sweet water! It's just not fair!"

David's three mighty friends heard him say that. They started talking quietly where David couldn't hear them.

"Do you think we could do it?" Shammah asked.

"We'd have to fight their whole stinking army," said Eleazar. "If we could sneak past their guards, we could make it to the well. Problem is, when we got there, they'd probably figure out we were the enemy. We'd be surrounded! We'd have to fight our way out. On the other hand, if we didn't sneak past the guards, we'd have to fight our way in *and* out! I'm not sure that's possible. We could all die for a cup of water."

"True," said Sharp Spear, "but think of the talk if we could pull it off! We march right into the middle of the Philistine army, take a cup of water, and march out with it. No one would be crazy enough to try this but us. Just think of the expression on David's face when we give it to him!"

"There's one more problem," moaned Shammah. "How could we keep a cup of water from spilling while we fight off hundreds of Philistines and climb back up this mountain? Even if we live, the water would probably spill out. It's not good to risk our lives and return with an empty cup!"

"That," said Eleazar, "is your problem. Let's go!"

Off they went. They snuck down the mountain. They made it into Bethlehem. They snuck past the guards all the way to the well. Then someone yelled, "Spies! Israelites! Get 'em!" The battle began. The Three covered the cup of water and drew their swords. Slowly, deliberately, risking their lives to save the water, they fought their way out of Bethlehem and back to the mountain. They climbed back up to the caves. By God's grace, the water stayed in the cup! By God's grace, they lived!

David couldn't believe it! His entire army couldn't believe it! The Philistines couldn't believe it! I'm not sure the three mighty friends could believe it. They risked their lives to bring their friend a glass of water. Their friendship was worth the risk.

What do you think David did with the water? Did he drink it? Did he share it with his three mighty friends? Nope, he poured it out on the dirt! Any idea why he did that?

David was so touched by what his friends did that he poured the water out as a gift to God. David didn't drink this water because it represented to him the life of his friends. To risk their lives to bring him water was more than he could imagine. So he offered the water to God.

Three people almost died for one cup of water. That's the world's most expensive water.

Remember: You've Got His Word on It

Jesus calls himself your friend. What do you suppose he means by that? What has he done for you? How can you act like a friend of his?

A friend is always loyal, and a brother is born to help in time of need. . . . There are "friends" who destroy each other, but a real friend sticks closer than a brother. . . . As iron sharpens iron, a friend sharpens a friend. Proverbs 17:17; 18:24; 27:17

Whether we are high above the sky or in the deepest ocean, nothing in all creation will ever be able to separate us from the love of God that is revealed in Christ Jesus our Lord. Romans 8:39

It is God who saved us and chose us to live a holy life. He did this not because we deserved it, but because that was his plan long before the world began—to show his love and kindness to us through Christ Jesus. 2 Timothy 1:9

9

She Couldn't Hide from a Blind Man

Scripture Passage: 1 Kings 14:1–20

So What? Don't try to trick God!

For Parents: [Anything in brackets]

Do any of your friends have names that are hard to pronounce? What are they? Any friends or kids in the same family with names that are almost identical? What are they?

This story has some tricky names in it. We'll change the names a little bit to make it easier to understand.

First, we have King Jeroboam. We'll call him King Jay. Next, we have King Jay's son called Abijah [Ah-bee-yah']. We'll call him Prince Bee. Then we have another name almost identical to the king's son's name, Prince Bee. There is a prophet of God called Ahijah [Akh-ee-yah']. We'll call him Pastor Eeee. Finally, we have King Jay's wife. The Bible doesn't give us her name; it simply refers to her as Jeroboam's wife. Since that's the only name we have for her in the Bible, we'll just call her Queen Jay.

> Have you ever been sick? I mean super-mega-feel-awful-sick?
> What did you do to get well?

King Jay was a bad king. He didn't want to follow God, and he didn't even try. King Jay loved to sin and worship false gods. One day something horrible happened to the king. His son Prince Bee [probably a young boy] became sick. He was sick for a long time, and he wasn't getting any better. Nothing seemed to work. The king and queen prayed to their false gods, but it didn't help.

King Jay knew that the true God could help his son. The problem was King Jay wouldn't pray to God. Jay wanted life his own way, and he knew that God would want him to change. He could ask Pastor Eeee to pray for his son, but King Jay had made life miserable for Pastor Eeee. In fact, King Jay made life miserable for almost anyone who worshipped the true God. If the people in town knew that King Jay wanted Pastor Eeee's help, they would know that the gods the king worshipped were fake. Then King Jay had an idea. It was a brilliant, terrible idea.

> What trick have you played on your friends? What trick do you
> think King Jay wants to play on Pastor Eeee?

King Jay didn't want anyone to see him go to Pastor Eeee for help, but he had no one else to go to. King Jay knew that Pastor Eeee liked to pray for people and help others. He also knew that Pastor Eeee was blind. The king would trick Pastor Eeee into praying for his son. No one would know that King Jay had gone to Pastor Eeee if he could do it in secret. King Jay went to talk to his queen.

King and Queen Jay quickly put their plan together. She changed out of her royal clothes into old street clothes. She made herself look different. Maybe she changed her hair color or wore a wig. She probably looked dirty or poor. What would you have done? Whatever she did, it was a great disguise. No one could recognize her as the queen now. She took gifts for Pastor Eeee so she could bribe him into praying for her son Prince Bee. Queen Jay left for Pastor Eeee's house. Would she make it without being recognized?

What do you do to help around the house? Does your family ever help other people? Whom would it be wrong to help?

The disguise worked! Queen Jay made it all the way to Pastor Eeee's house without anyone knowing who she was! Queen Jay thought her husband would be proud. The rest should be easy. At least Pastor Eeee was blind. Still, she was scared. Her heart was beating fast when she arrived at Pastor Eeee's door. All she needed to do was to have him pray for her son. If she could get him to say that Prince Bee would be all right, then she could run home knowing her son would be okay. God always seemed to answer Pastor Eeee's prayers. She was almost there. Her disguise needed to work for just a few more seconds. Then she would be in the house with the blind pastor, and no one could recognize her. She reached for the door. She knocked.

"Come in, Queen Jay!" said Pastor Eeee.

"Nooo!" she thought. "How could Pastor Eeee know? My disguise was perfect! He's blind! Who told him? How come I couldn't hide from a blind man?"

King and Queen Jay wanted to trick God into helping them. Instead, God tricked the king and queen by telling Pastor Eeee who was coming. They wanted to trick God, but God tricked them! Queen Jay probably walked home slowly and sadly because Pastor Eeee wouldn't pray for her son or bless her family. She desired wickedness more than God's blessing.

Why did Queen Jay disguise herself? Why did she need to hide who she really was? It was because she and her husband were disobeying God. God helps us when we give our lives to him. You cannot trick God into helping you. He knows who you really are. No matter what disguise you put on, no matter what you wear, God still knows who you are. If you reject God like the king and queen did, he will reject you. It's no use trying to trick God. That will never work! What works is to accept him. If you follow him, he will help you, as he helped Pastor Eeee.

Remember: You've Got His Word on It

In Psalm 34 King David talks to children [see verse 11, the word translated "children" can mean "young ones, child, or grandchild"] about trusting in God.

I will boast only in the LORD; let all who are discouraged take heart. Come, let us tell of the Lord's greatness; let us exalt his name together. I prayed to the LORD, and he answered me, freeing me from all my fears.

For the angel of the LORD guards all who fear him, and he rescues them. Taste and see that the LORD is good. Oh, the joys of those who trust in him!

Come, my children, and listen to me, and I will teach you to fear the LORD. Do any of you want to live a life that is long and good? Then watch your tongue! Keep your lips from telling lies! Turn away from evil and do good. Work hard at living in peace with others. The eyes of the LORD watch over those who do right; his ears are open to their cries for help. But the LORD turns his face against those who do evil; he will erase their memory from the earth. The LORD hears his people when they call to him for help. He rescues them from all their troubles.

Psalm 34:2–4, 7–8, 11–17

He Kills Four Hundred Men and Runs from One Woman

Scripture Passage: 1 Kings 18–19

So What? Power comes from faith in God; panic comes from faith in us!

For Parents: [Anything in brackets]

> Why would anyone need to kill four hundred men? What do you think it was like to worship idols and other false gods in Old Testament times?

In the land of Israel, when Ahab was king, the people once again forgot about God. They were worshipping idols. Usually they worshipped them up high on a mountain. They thought they were closer to the gods that way. Sometimes they would worship a god called Baal.

Can you say Baal? *Baal* is an old Hebrew word for god. However, Baal was a false god.

Almost everybody was worshipping false gods. What would it be like to live at that time? What might you do?

There was one man who said, "This has to stop!" This man was a prophet of God. He said to the people, "You have a Baal god that you worship on Mount Carmel. He's called the god of rain and thunder and lightning. Here's what I am doing. I'm challenging the god of lightning to a showdown!" You probably know this part of the story, but you might not know the end of the story. Keep listening; we'll get to it! The prophet's name was Elijah. He had faith in God and didn't seem to be afraid of anything.

The false prophets gathered on Mount Carmel. There were 450 prophets of Baal and 400 other false prophets who worshipped with a wicked woman named Jezebel, the wife of King Ahab. Can you say Jezebel? She was about as nice as her name! Now it was Elijah and his God against 850 false prophets and their demons. It took a lot of faith for Elijah to fight against that many enemies at once.

How do you think Elijah felt? Do you remember what Elijah did?

Elijah ordered two bulls to be brought to Mount Carmel, one for Baal and one for God. So there they were: 850 prophets who worshipped Baal up on the mountain. Elijah challenged them to call fire [probably in the form of lightning] down from heaven. It is quite possible that they could do that. They may have even done that before. But Elijah knew that the true God was more powerful than a zillion false prophets.

The false prophets ran around the mountain; they called, they yelled, and they did other stuff. Did the lightning come down and burn up their sacrifice? Nope. Why couldn't they bring down lightning this time? Because God and his angels stopped them from bringing lightning down! Elijah was making fun of them when they tried to make fire come down. He yelled, "Shout louder! Maybe your god's thinking too hard and he can't hear. Or maybe he's on a trip, so you need to yell louder." He also said, "Maybe your god is in the bathroom!" Did Elijah really say that? Yes, he did! So they kept shouting, but there was no response; no one answered.

Finally, they gave up. Elijah was confident. He had the people watch him as he rebuilt the altar of the Lord that had been torn down. He had them watch as he poured water all over the altar. Then they heard him pray. He didn't shout. He didn't yell. He just prayed. And what do you suppose happened? The fire came down!

All the people who had come to watch the showdown started screaming, "Jehovah is God! Jehovah is God!" Do you know what Elijah did? He yelled, "Grab the prophets of Baal! Don't let any of them get away!"

So the people grabbed the prophets of Baal. And Elijah obeyed God's order to kill them all. Elijah was the most powerful man in the world that day.

Have you ever felt great one day and lousy the next? When was that? Have you ever felt strong and fast one day and weak or slow the next? Have you ever been in a panic? Ever fall into the deep end of a pool or get lost somewhere?

The Bible tells us Queen Jezebel was furious when she heard that Elijah killed the false prophets. They were her friends. Now she was mad at Elijah, and she promised she would kill him that very day.

So Elijah ran.

Why did Elijah run from one woman? [Panic.] Who protected Elijah up on the mountain? Was it because Elijah was so big and so strong that 850 false prophets couldn't hurt him? Who protected him? Could God protect Elijah from Jezebel? Then why should he run?

The strongest man in the world that day was Elijah. Then he acted like a wimp! In one day, he went from strong to weak. Elijah forgot who protected him on the mountain. Maybe he started thinking he defeated the false prophets all by himself. One thing is for certain, he lost his faith in God. That's what made him panic. That's what turned him into a wimp. You can be sure God wasn't afraid of Jezebel. God took care of Jezebel later. You can read that story in 2 Kings 9.

God is strong. He can do powerful things through you, if you have faith in him. God was with Elijah, and he can be with you too. Our power comes from faith in God. Panic comes from faith in us.

Remember: You've Got His Word on It

I no longer count on my own goodness or my ability to obey God's law, but I trust Christ to save me. For God's way of making us right with himself depends on faith. As a result, I can really know Christ and experience the mighty power that raised him from the dead. . . . And God, in his mighty power, will protect you until you receive this salvation, because you are trusting him. It will be revealed on the last day for all to see. Philippians 3:9–10; 1 Peter 1:5

— II —
God of the Flies

Scripture Passage: 2 Kings 1

So What? You should disobey people when they want you to disobey God!

For Parents: [Anything in brackets]

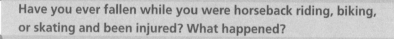

Have you ever fallen while you were horseback riding, biking, or skating and been injured? What happened?

Do you remember our last story? It was about King Ahab, Queen Jezebel, and the prophet Elijah. Now King Ahab has died, and there is a new king in the land. His name is Ahaziah [pronounced Akh-az-yaw']. We'll call him "Ah-ah-sneeze."

One day King Ah-ah-sneeze was relaxing in his big chair in front of the window. Suddenly he leaned too far back. The window broke, and he fell through to the floor below! [Your Bible probably says he fell through the lattice of his upper room. Lattice was used to cover window openings for safety and to allow air to circulate in the rooms.] He was hurt badly, and the doctors didn't know if he would live or die.

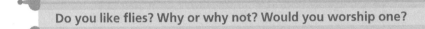

Do you like flies? Why or why not? Would you worship one?

The doctors couldn't help King Ah-ah-sneeze, so he decided to ask his false god for help. He knew he should consult the true God, but he didn't want to. So he called for his messengers and said to them, "Go consult god Baal-zebub [pronounced Bah'-al zeb-oob'] to see whether I will live or die!"

Can you say Baal-zebub? Baal means "god" and Zebub means "flies." Therefore, he said, "Go consult the god of flies to see whether I will live or die!" [Some think the translation should be Baal-Zebul, which means God Exalted. However, they're in the minority, and this makes for a better story, so I'm sticking with it!]

When Elijah the prophet heard that King Ah-ah-sneeze was going to the god of the flies, he was mad, very mad. The king of Israel was supposed to worship the one true God and God only. The god of the flies was not God!

Elijah found the messengers on the way to the temple. They should not have obeyed the king and gone to the temple of the god of the flies. The true God wouldn't want them doing this. Elijah asked them, "Why are you going to the god of the flies? Don't you believe in the one true God of Israel? Because of this, King Ah-ah-sneeze will die."

And what did they do? They ran back to the king, of course, and told him what happened. The king got very mad. He was sick. He was hurt. And he wanted the help of the god of the flies!

What do you do when you get mad? What do your parents do when they get angry? [Sorry, kind of.]

King Ah-ah-sneeze sent an army captain with fifty soldiers to arrest Elijah. If Elijah wouldn't let him consult with the god of the flies, he would take Elijah out of the way. With Elijah in jail, the king could send his messengers to the god of the flies and get his god to help. What he told this captain and fifty soldiers to do was sin. They shouldn't arrest Elijah. But they obeyed King Ah-ah-sneeze and disobeyed God. When the captain and soldiers found Elijah sitting on a hill, they yelled to him, "Man of God! The king says get down here now!"

Did they really think Elijah was a man of God? No. So what they were really saying was, "Hey, you who think you are a man of God! King Ah-ah-sneeze says get down here right now. You're under arrest!" No doubt, they all had their weapons with them—swords, shields, bows, and arrows.

Elijah wasn't afraid of the captain, or his army, or the king. Elijah said, "If I really am a man of God, fire will come down from heaven and burn you up."

What happened? Fire came down from heaven and burned them up! They should have obeyed God rather than the king.

Can you guess what sick King Ah-ah-sneeze did next? He sent another captain with another fifty soldiers to arrest Elijah! Whom do you think they will obey, God or the king? Well, this captain said the same thing as the first one: "Hey, you who think you are a man of God! King Ah-ah-sneeze says get down here right now. You're under arrest!"

What do you think Elijah said back to him? Right, the same thing he said before: "If I really am a man of God, fire will come down from heaven and burn you up."

What happened? Yup, they burned up too!

When is it okay to disobey an adult? When is it okay to disobey your parents?

Then King Ah-ah-sneeze sent a third captain with fifty more men. Do you wonder if the king doesn't learn very fast? Maybe he doesn't like his captains or his soldiers. He's somewhat slow, don't you think? Maybe when the king fell, he hit his head.

What do you think the third captain said to Elijah? He said something different than the first two captains. This captain got on his knees and begged, "Man of God, please spare my life! And please spare the lives of the fifty men who came with me!" He had more respect for God than for the king. He knew whom to obey.

The angel of the Lord spoke to Elijah and said, "Go, Elijah. Go ahead and go with this captain. Go see King Ah-ah-sneeze. You don't have to be afraid."

Elijah went with the captain and the fifty soldiers to see the king. He told the king that he should not have sent messengers to the god of the flies. Only the one true God has the power of life and death. Then he told King Ah-ah-sneeze that he would die.

Verse 17 of 2 Kings 1 says what happened next. "He died." That was that. But who lived? Elijah who followed God lived. The captain who obeyed God lived. The fifty soldiers who followed the captain who obeyed God lived.

Only those who followed the god of the flies died. In addition, those who followed King Ah-ah-sneeze who followed the god of the flies died. Whenever someone tells you to do something different from what God says to do, you should disobey! You must disobey them in order to obey God.

Remember: You've Got His Word on It

If they listen and obey God, then they will be blessed with prosperity throughout their lives. All their years will be pleasant. Job 36:11

But Peter and the apostles replied, "We must obey God rather than human authority." Acts 5:29

See to it that you obey God, the one who is speaking to you. For if the people of Israel did not escape when they refused to listen to Moses, the earthly messenger, how terrible our danger if we reject the One who speaks to us from heaven! Hebrews 12:25

Obey God because you are his children. 1 Peter 1:14

12

Don't Call This Man Baldy

Scripture Passage: 2 Kings 2:23–24

So What? God promises to protect you!

For Parents: [Anything in brackets]

> Do you remember your first day at camp? Do you remember your first day at school or Sunday school in a new church? What was it like?

This story, which is only two verses long, is about a new young prophet named Elisha. Elisha was about twenty-five years old. His best friend, Elijah, had been a prophet too, but now Elijah was gone. God had picked Elijah up in a chariot, and they had blasted off to heaven. Now Elisha had to take Elijah's place. This was a very important job, and Elisha might have been a little scared to begin his first day. This would be the perfect chance for Satan to pick on him.

Elisha was walking down a road when a gang of bullies started mocking him. About fifty tough-looking guys started circling around him. [If you are using the KJV Bible, it says that they were "little children." The Hebrew word actually refers to young men between the ages of twelve and thirty. It's just my guess that there were at least fifty of them. We know that the bears mauled forty-two. It seems logical to me that some got away while the bears were busy with the others, so there could have been many more.]

What is a bully? What is it like to have someone pick on you? What are some mean things that bullies do to people now?

You can imagine this large gang of young men closing in on Elisha. They probably had rocks and hard sticks to use as weapons. They definitely had wicked smiles on their faces. Being alone, Elisha had nowhere to run, no way to defend himself against so many. First, they started making fun of him.

They yelled things like, "Hey, baldy, why don't you go blast up like your friend did? If you're really a prophet, why can't you go too?" They didn't call him baldy because he was bald. Elisha was probably too young for that, and men in those days wore things on their heads (like big cloth hats) so you couldn't see their hair anyway. They didn't know if he had hair or not. Calling someone bald was just a way to make fun of him or her. At that time most of the bald men were those who had to shave their heads because of a sickness called leprosy. So, these bullies were yelling, "Hey, are you sick in the head

or what? Do you really think you're a prophet? What's so great about a bald prophet who can't even blast away? You don't look so tough with all of us around you!"

> When you're scared, who do you want walking by your side? Who would you like to keep bullies away from you?

Elisha turned around and looked at them. He said something like, "I'll let God protect me. God can take care of you!"

Then God did something he had promised to do many years before. He said, "If you remain hostile toward me and refuse to listen to me, . . . I will send wild animals against you, and they will rob you of your children" (Lev. 26:21–22 NIV). Immediately two bears came flying out of the woods! The bullies screamed and ran, but they couldn't run fast enough. The bears flew after them. When the bullies ran faster, the bears ran faster still. The bears mauled forty-two of the young men. Evidently, God doesn't like bullies either!

Elisha didn't run. He knew God had sent the bears and he wouldn't be hurt. He just continued on his way down the road.

Sometimes God protects us by sending angels or friends. Sometimes God protects us by bringing us home to himself. God protected Elisha by sending wild animals to fight for him.

Remember: You've Got His Word on It

Can you remember any places in the Bible when God promises to protect you or others? Here are a few:

God is my rock, in whom I find protection. He is my shield, the strength of my salvation, and my stronghold, my high tower, my savior, the one who saves me from violence. 2 Samuel 22:3

As for God, his way is perfect. All the LORD's promises prove true. He is a shield for all who look to him for protection. 2 Samuel 22:31

The LORD is my rock, my fortress, and my savior; my God is my rock, in whom I find protection. He is my shield, the strength of my salvation, and my stronghold. Psalm 18:2

Every word of God proves true. He defends all who come to him for protection. Proverbs 30:5

13

The Disease That Jumps

Scripture Passage: 2 Kings 5

So What? Sin has a price, and you don't want to pay it!

For Parents: [Anything in brackets]

Have you ever heard of a disease jumping? Have you ever caught a cold from another person? Have you ever given the flu to someone in your family? [Those germs jumped!]

This story isn't about just passing a cold bug from one person to another. Nope, not even close. It's about a disease that jumped from one person to another! And this is one disease you don't want to get.

This disease that jumped is a skin disease called leprosy. [The Hebrew word translated "leprosy" in your Bible could also refer to other skin diseases as well.] Leprosy has been around a long time, and at one time it affected every part of the world, all seven continents. It's a horrible disease. Leprosy makes you itch, and it destroys your skin. In time it can spread over your whole body. It was even worse in Bible times because there was no cure for it. Eventually, leprosy would kill you. Today we have treatment for leprosy, but not everyone can afford the treatment. Even today, there are over a million people suffering with leprosy.

> Do you know anyone in the army? Do you know what a general is? What does a general do?

Naaman was a general in the army. His king liked him a lot because he had won a lot of battles. Naaman's problem was that he had leprosy. [In Israel, he would have been isolated, but that was not always the case in other countries. Naaman was from Aram, where lepers were allowed to associate with other people.] Naaman had a girl working for him who knew Elisha. The girl knew Elisha was a prophet of God and that God could cure leprosy, so she told Naaman about Elisha.

Now, tell me everything you know about Naaman: [He is a general, so he's probably wealthy. The king likes him, so he's powerful. He has a girl working for him who knows Elisha. This gives him insight into what the prophet can do for him. And he has leprosy.]

> Could Naaman go to a doctor to cure his leprosy? What would you do if you were Naaman? How much would you pay to be cured?

Naaman went to Elisha. He took lots of money with him to pay Elisha for his help. He even had a letter from the king asking for help. Naaman put his money in the chariot, the letter in his pocket, and went to see Elisha.

Knock! Knock! Knock! Naaman pounded on Elisha's door. "Hey!" he probably yelled, "I'm General Naaman! I've come to see Elisha! I have a note from the king asking you to cure me of my leprosy! I brought clothes and money for you, and I want to be cured!"

Did Elisha go talk to him? Nope. He sent his servant out! Who goes to greet the important, powerful General Naaman at the door? The proud general is greeted by—a servant! Wow, was the general mad! Then Elisha's servant said, "Go and wash seven times in the Jordan River, and your leprosy will go away." Now the Jordan River was, and still is, a filthy, dirty river. Who washes in dirty water? If sores and cuts covered your body, would you want to go wash in dirty water? Can you imagine your mother filling up the tub with mud, then putting in some water, and saying, "Okay, time for your bath!"

First Elisha didn't even come out to talk to Naaman. Then a servant told him to bathe in dirty water.

Naaman was angry. "I thought he was going to come out and talk to me," said Naaman. "Then he would pray to his God, and he would wave his hands over the spots of leprosy and cure me. Who does Elisha think he is anyway? The rivers back home are cleaner than any rivers here in Israel. I can wash in them if I want to wash in a river." He grabbed his sword and stomped off in a rage.

Naaman's servants went to him and said, "Please, Naaman, if this prophet has told you to do it, why not at least try it?" So Naaman, even though he was angry, listened to his servants. He went in the dirty, muddy, stinky, filthy Jordan River and took his dirt bath.

When he came out, his skin looked as clean and fresh as a young boy's. He was sure glad he obeyed God!

The leprosy was gone! How could a dirty river cure him of a horrible deadly disease? It didn't. God did. God had Naaman bathe in a dirty river to prove that the river didn't cure him. God cured him!

How do you think Naaman felt? What would you do now if you were him? If you were rich, what would you buy your family for Christmas?

Naaman was so happy that he went right back to Elisha's house. He tried to pay Elisha for getting him healed. Elisha knew that he hadn't done anything; God had made Naaman well. Elisha wouldn't take any of Naaman's gifts. The cure was free! [Wow, is it possible—a free doctor?] The only cost was for Naaman to have faith in God and obey him by bathing in the river. The river didn't cure him. Elisha didn't cure him. God cured him.

What is greed? Why is it bad? Have you ever wanted something so badly that you would do something wrong to get it?

Elisha had a servant named Gehazi. Gehazi was greedy. He said to himself, "Self," he said, "I think Elisha was too easy on Naaman. He should have charged him for healing him. Naaman has plenty of money and clothing. I help Elisha, so maybe some of those gifts should be mine. I'll go find Naaman and tell him that he needs to pay us for being cured." So Gehazi found Naaman, and Naaman gave him clothing and two bags of money for the cure. But Gehazi didn't cure Naaman, God did.

Then something happened. The disease jumped! The skin disease that Naaman had before jumped to Gehazi! Now Gehazi had Naaman's leprosy! And he had it until the day he died.

Naaman trusted and obeyed God, and his leprosy went away. Gehazi was greedy, he disobeyed God, and leprosy came to him. Trusting and obeying God as Naaman did is free. Greed, like all sin, has a price.

Remember: You've Got His Word on It

You will be accepted if you respond in the right way. But if you refuse to respond correctly, then watch out! Sin is waiting to attack and destroy you, and you must subdue it. Genesis 4:7

So just as sin ruled over all people and brought them to death, now God's wonderful kindness rules instead, giving us right standing with God and resulting in eternal life through Jesus Christ our Lord. Romans 5:21

Don't you realize that whatever you choose to obey becomes your master? You can choose sin, which leads to death, or you can choose to obey God and receive his approval. Romans 6:16

When someone sins, he earns what sin pays—death. But God gives us a free gift—life forever in Christ Jesus our Lord. Romans 6:23 ICB

---------— 14 ——————

The Invisible Army That Was

Scripture Passage: 2 Kings 6:8–23

So What? God is invisible, and he's working in your life!

For Parents: [Anything in brackets]

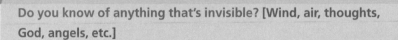

Do you know of anything that's invisible? [Wind, air, thoughts, God, angels, etc.]

The king of Syria hated Israel. He wanted to kill the people and destroy the entire country. Israel knew they were in danger from Syria. Problem was, there wasn't much they could do about it. Syria had a large army and attacked Israel whenever they had a chance. Only one thing was keeping Israel from being overrun by Syria.

What is military intelligence? Why do you think it would be important in wartime?

Military intelligence was the one thing keeping Israel safe from Syria. All the intelligence was coming from one prophet of God, Elisha. God was telling Elisha everything Syria was doing, and that kept Israel safe.

If the king of Syria tried to trap Israel's army in a canyon, Elisha would know. He would tell Israel's army, and they would hike around the canyon. If Syria tried to launch a surprise attack, it was no surprise to Israel. Even if the king of Syria whispered secrets to his generals in his bedroom, Elisha and all Israel would know! The king of Syria kept trying to fight Israel, but Israel kept moving around them. That's how God kept Israel safe.

If you were the king of Syria, what would you think was happening? [Spies.] How could Israel know so much? What would you do about it?

"So," the king of Syria thought, "there must be a spy in my midst. Someone is telling the king of Israel what's happening. There's a spy! Who is it?"

The king questioned his army. "Where have you been? You aren't a spy, are you? Who were you talking to last night? Where were you yesterday?" He hunted and hunted, but he found no spies. Why couldn't he find the spies? Were there spies in his camp? No!

One of his officers went to the king and said, "O King, live forever! You keep looking for a spy in the camp, but there isn't one. What's happening is Elisha, the prophet in Israel, tells the king of Israel everything—even the words you say in your bedroom!"

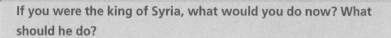

The king was extremely mad. His face became red, and he said, "If Elisha is the cause of this, we must get him! Go now! Hunt down Elisha and tell me where he is. Then I will send my army to capture him. Once I have him, I will take over Israel."

The men found out Elisha was in Dothan. The king of Syria quickly sent a huge force of horses and chariots to Dothan before Elisha could leave. Instead of going in the daytime, they snuck in at night and surrounded the whole city of Dothan. Elisha was trapped! The evil king had him right where he wanted him.

Elisha had a servant with him. The servant got up early in the morning and saw an entire army of horses and chariots surrounding the city. He quickly woke up Elisha and yelled, "Elisha! Elisha! What are we going to do?"

What do you think Elisha did?

Elisha told his servant, "Don't be afraid. There are more of us than there are of them."

How many of "us" were there? Two!

How many of "them" were there? Hundreds!

What in the world was Elisha talking about? Didn't he know how to count? Then Elisha prayed, "O LORD! Open my servant's eyes so he can see what I can see!"

What did Elisha mean? His friend wasn't blind. He could see as well as you and I. Elisha, being a prophet, could see things you, his servant, and I couldn't see. Elisha could see the invisible things God was doing.

God answered Elisha's prayer. He opened the servant's eyes so he could see what Elisha could see. Immediately the servant saw the hills full of horses and chariots of fire. There were angels all around Elisha. There were more angels around Elisha than there were people in Syria's army. Wow! Wouldn't that be cool to see? God is always doing things we can't see. It would be easier to trust him if we could see all the things he's doing. But he always asks us to trust him even though we are blind to what he's doing.

So the enemies from Syria came toward Elisha and his servant. Was the servant afraid of the enemy anymore? No way! Could the enemy see the angels? Nope; they thought they had Elisha and his servant outnumbered. The Syrian army couldn't see God's invisible army!

Elisha now asked God for the angels' help. If you were Elisha, what would you ask the angels to do?

Elisha asked God to have the angels make every person in the Syrian army blind. Now they not only couldn't see the angels, they couldn't see Elisha and his servant. The entire world was now invisible to them; they couldn't see a thing! They didn't know God had an entire army of angels working against them.

Elisha and his servant went out to speak to the blind army. The conversation probably went something like this.

"Hey, are you guys okay? You look like you're lost or something."

"Help us, please! Something happened—a bright light, a flash, something; anyway, we're all blind now!"

"Where are you from? Where are you going? We'll help you if we can," said Elisha, with a smile on his face.

"We're the Syrian army. We were looking for a man named Elisha, to take him back to our king. We heard he was here in Dothan."

"I can help you find Elisha," said Elisha. "I know him well. Just follow me, and I'll take you to him. I can even make sure you get back home safely."

"Wow, I can't believe it. Thanks; I don't know what we'd do without you."

"Here, take my hand," I'll lead you where you need to go." So Elisha led the blind army out of Dothan. A silly looking army they must have been, probably holding hands so they wouldn't get lost or left behind, tripping over rocks and roots. That must be how we look to the angels when we live without following God. We make mistakes, get lost, and trip over our sin. We're blind without God.

It took some time before Elisha had the army where he wanted them. He brought the Syrian army right to the Israelite army and their king. He captured an entire army all by himself! Well—he did have a little help from the angels.

Then Elisha prayed, "LORD, open their eyes so they can see." What do you think they saw? God didn't let them see the angels, but he did let them see as everyone else could see. They saw the Israelites surrounding them. They saw Elisha, whom they were looking for, standing in front of them. Elisha was their guide! "Wow, were we dumb," they must have thought. And they saw Elisha's servant. Then they saw the king of Israel.

> What should the king of Israel do with the Syrian army? What would you do?

The Syrians must have been surprised to go blind. They must have been even more surprised to find out that their guide had been the very man they were looking for—Elisha. Now they would have an even greater surprise.

The Syrians were surprised *and* scared. Since they had made a life out of killing Israelites, they were afraid the Israelites would kill or torture them.

The king of Israel asked Elisha, "Should I kill the Syrians? Shall I kill them, Elisha? Can I, can I?" It was then that the Syrians had their greatest surprise of the day. Elisha answered, "No. There's no need to kill anybody. They're prisoners. You don't kill prisoners, even in war. Instead, give them food and water so they can eat and drink. Then let them go! Send them back home to Syria."

The king prepared a huge meal for the captured soldiers. What a surprise! After the soldiers finished eating and drinking, the king of Israel sent them back home to Syria. From that time on, Syria stopped their evil ways of troubling Israel. They knew there was no way to defeat an invisible army!

God surprises us the same way. When we blindly follow our sin and trip over ourselves, he offers forgiveness. We can't see him, but we know he's working just the same. No matter where we are or what we've done, God and his angels are working to bring us back to him. He's invisible, and he's working in your life and mine!

Remember: You've Got His Word on It

Joseph: The LORD was with Joseph and blessed him greatly as he served in the home of his Egyptian master. . . . But the LORD was with Joseph [in jail], too, and he granted Joseph favor with the chief jailer. Genesis 39:2, 21

Jonah: Now the LORD had arranged for a great fish to swallow Jonah. And Jonah was inside the fish for three days and three nights. Jonah 1:17

Baruch and Jeremiah: Then the king commanded his son
Jerahmeel, Seraiah son of Azriel, and Shelemiah son of Abdeel
to arrest Baruch and Jeremiah. But the LORD had hidden them.
Jeremiah 36:26

Mary and Joseph: But when it was time to leave, they went
home another way, because God had warned them in a dream
not to return to Herod. After the wise men were gone, an angel
of the Lord appeared to Joseph in a dream. "Get up and flee to
Egypt with the child and his mother," the angel said. "Stay there
until I tell you to return, because Herod is going to try to kill
the child." Matthew 2:12–13

Me and you: God alone made it possible for you to be in Christ
Jesus. For our benefit God made Christ to be wisdom itself.
He is the one who made us acceptable to God. He made us
pure and holy, and he gave himself to purchase our freedom.
1 Corinthians 1:30

15

The Loud Army That Wasn't

Scripture Passage: 2 Kings 6:24–7:20

So What? God keeps all his promises!

For Parents: [Anything in brackets]

Tell about the worst food you've ever eaten. How did it taste?

This story begins with a war for the city called Samaria. Samaria, like most cities in Bible times, had walls around it for protection. The families would live inside the walls, in the city. During the day they would leave the walls to work in the farms outside the city. At night they would return inside the walls where it was safe. You could say they had morning and evening rush hours like we do. In the morning, everyone was leaving the city. At nighttime, the gate was busy with everyone coming back home.

Now I want you to pretend you are a wicked king. Make the meanest-looking face you can. Your name is King Ben-Hadad, and you are at war with Samaria. Samaria had a strong defense. The wall around it was twenty to thirty feet thick. That's thick enough to drive three cars side-by-side on top of the wall! Besides that, the city was built on a hill three hundred feet high. That is about as high as [pick a thirty-story building in town, or maybe fifteen houses on top of each other]

Now, how would you take over this city? What ideas do you have? Noooo, you can't do that! Remember, this is 2,700 years ago! You can't use planes, tanks, or guns. You can only use swords, slings, arrows, spears, and weapons you can make. So do you have any other ideas?

The wicked king had a special way he wanted to take Samaria. He wanted to win without having even one of his men die. Before you know *how* he planned to do this, you first need to know *why* he wanted to do it. He didn't really care about taking over Samaria. He was after just one man who lived there. That man was Elisha, a man who followed God. King Ben-Hadad didn't like that, and he wanted Elisha dead. The problem was that Samaria was protecting Elisha, so King Ben-Hadad had to attack the entire city. Any idea yet how he did it without risking any men?

Ben-Hadad decided to surround Samaria. That way no one could go into or out of the city. He had a huge army, so they made a circle around the city. If people left through the city gate, his army would kill them. If people stayed in the city too long, they would run out of food, because the farms were outside the city.

So King Ben-Hadad surrounded Samaria. He and his army then sat outside the city and waited. They played cards. They waited. They ate pizza. They waited some more. They ate chocolate cake. Then they waited a little longer.

What do you think was happening inside the city?

Inside Samaria, the people were becoming hungry, and hungrier, and hungrier. They became so hungry that they even ate donkey heads. Yuck! What do you think they tasted like? People were even scraping up bird droppings and selling them for food. Yuckier! [Is that a word?] I don't even want to know what that tasted like. Finally, the king of Israel gave up because his people were starving. He ordered his messenger to kill Elisha. He thought if Elisha was dead, King Ben-Hadad would leave them alone.

When the messenger went to kill Elisha, Elisha was at home. We don't know exactly how, but somehow God told Elisha that the messenger was coming to kill him. God also told Elisha that there would be plenty of food in the city the very next day. What would you do if you knew someone was coming to your house to hurt you? Well, Elisha and his friends quickly locked the doors. Then the messenger showed up. Elisha told the messenger that there would be lots and lots of food the next day. The messenger didn't believe him. He said that couldn't happen even if God made it rain food down from heaven. The messenger wasn't too bright about believing God. Elisha told the messenger, "Because you don't believe God, you will see the food but not get to eat any of it." Wouldn't that be awful? Wouldn't you hate to be starving and see tons and tons of food and not get to eat any of it?

What scares you? Do you ever have nightmares?

Okay, pretend you're King Ben-Hadad with the mean face again. It's nighttime, and you're sleeping in your tent. You are with your army in a big circle around Samaria. You have lookouts to make sure no one sneaks out of the city. Suddenly you wake up out of a nightmare. You hear the most terrifying sound on the earth. Immediately you feel both sick and scared. You hear the Hittites! Your nightmare is real!

The Hittites were the fiercest army around. Everyone was afraid of them. They had fast chariots pulled by powerful horses that would run right over people. On the wheels of their chariots were swords that stuck out and made a loud whirling noise when they cut through the air. Have you ever heard one of those planes with the propellers in the front? That's kind of what they sounded like. The Hittites could run people over with their horses or cut people with the swords coming out of their chariot wheels. They could run right over a tent, killing everyone inside.

There you are sound asleep in your tent. Suddenly you wake up and hear the loud whirling noise of the Hittite swords spinning fast. The chariots are running toward your tent! There's no time to find your clothes. You run outside in your pajamas, and you hear the horses breathing hard. They must be just a few steps behind you! You dare not turn around. You run and run and run. The faster you run the closer they seem to come. You can almost feel the breath of the horses on your neck. Always the whirling sound of the swords fills the air. You run all night until all your strength is gone. Finally, you give up and fall to the ground to die. But no horse runs you over. No swords hurt you. You still hear them, but nothing happens. When you dare to, you look around, and you see . . . nothing!

There were no Hittites! That's right. God won the war with King Ben-Hadad by sound only. He simply put the sound of the Hittites into the ears of Ben-Hadad and his army. They were too scared to turn around. When they finally did, they saw . . . nothing! They had run all night and left everything. They left all their clothes, swords, horses, tents, and food for Elisha and his friends in Samaria. They had run from nothing but the sound of the power of God.

Do you remember the promise Elisha made to the king's messenger, the man who came to kill him? What was it? Right, he promised him that he would see the food but not get to eat any of it.

Soon someone noticed that King Ben-Hadad and his army were gone. The king of Israel then called the same messenger that he sent to kill Elisha. He said, "Because you're my most trusted servant, I put you in charge of opening the gate in our city walls. Then the entire city can go out and get the food King Ben-Hadad left." When the gate opened, the hungry people rushed out to the food. "Finally," the people thought, "something besides donkey heads and bird droppings!" The messenger opened the gate and saw the wonderful food. Then the Samaria rush hour began. The people rushing out of the city trampled the messenger. He saw the food but never ate any of it.

The promise of food was a wonderful promise. The messenger didn't believe God, so he didn't get to eat the food. That was sad. Each and every promise of God will come true. He always keeps his word. If we believe in him, his promises to us are great, never sad. Can you think of some of God's promises to you? Let's thank him for his promises.

Remember: You've Got His Word on It

God is the giver of good gifts (Matt. 7:11).

God washes away the sins of those who believe in him (Titus 3:4–6).

God gives wisdom (James 1:5).

God is love, and he loves those who love him (1 John 4:8).

God watches over his children (Matt. 18:10).

God forgives sins and gives his Holy Spirit to all who believe in him (Acts 2:38–39).

God will give the crown of life to those who love him (James 1:12).

God promises his kingdom to those who love him (James 2:5).

God promises eternal life (Titus 1:2).

God's promises all come true; none fail (Josh. 23:14).

God promises to come back again (2 Peter 3:4).

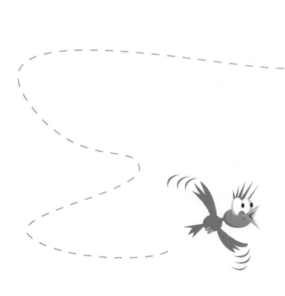

---- **16** ----

The Crazy King

Scripture Passage: Daniel 4

So What? God rules and gives kingdoms to whomever he wants!

For Parents: [Anything in brackets]

What does it mean to be crazy? [You don't know what is real anymore.] .

This is a story about crazy King Nebuchadnezzar. Can you say Nebuchadnezzar? How would you like that to be your name? What do you think the other kids would call you? We'll call him Neb. Here's what it means when we call Neb a crazy king. It means that he didn't know what was real anymore. Mixed up in the head for a while, that's what Neb was. First, I need to tell you a little about him. Babylon was the biggest city in the world, capital of the biggest empire in the world. And Neb was its king.

What's the difference between a king and a president or prime minister? [A king answers to no one. A king can do whatever he wants.] Can a prime minister or president do that? We elect our prime ministers and presidents by voting for them. Do you vote for a king?

Neb was the king, and at first he was following God. But the longer he was king, the farther he got from God. Have there been times when you weren't doing what you should do? When you got farther and farther from God? Well, that's what was happening to Neb. He wasn't following God anymore. Instead, he was doing his own thing. That's probably easy to do when you're king. Think about it. He was the richest, most powerful person in the world. He had more money than anybody else. [It's like a Bill Gates with endless money plus a dictator with endless power.] Wow. He could do whatever he wanted whenever he wanted. Neb could say, "I want to buy the Colorado Avalanche," and he could buy it. He could own the team. He could do whatever he wanted. He was powerful, and he had plenty of money. But he forgot that God is the true king. He forgot that God gives kingdoms to whomever he wants.

Have you ever had a dream that was super-real? One that was so real that when you woke up, the dream seemed more real than your bedroom?

Well, one day, Neb had one of those kind of dreams. Remember, things were going good for Neb, but he wasn't very close to God. This dream really, really bugged him. He thought it must have some special meaning, but no one could tell him what it meant.

Now, here is what he dreamt. In the dream, there was a tree. The tree grew bigger and bigger and bigger. Then it grew bigger again. Kind of like the beanstalk in "Jack and the Beanstalk." It was a huge tree. It was so big that almost wherever you were, you could see it. All the animals in the whole earth could sit under its shade. It was that big. Tons of birds were in it. It had all kinds of fruit so you could feed everyone in the world with its fruit. It was this massive big honking tree. Then an angel came down from heaven. The angel said, "Cut it down! Cut the branches off! Strip the leaves off! Throw out all the fruit! Knock it down and cut it off so that it's like a stump. Leave the roots in the ground and leave the stump, but cut everything else out."

Then the angel said something rather odd. He said, "The stump represents a person. I want that stump, that person, to think he's an animal. I want him to live with the cows and the dogs. I want that person to eat grass like a cow and walk on all fours like a dog." This person would have to live outside. His fingernails and toenails would grow long. He would have to eat grass. It would rain on him and snow on him. This person would really think he was an animal. The angel was saying, in effect, "He will go outside and think he's crazy. And I want this person to be out there and think he's crazy for seven long years!"

What do you think the dream meant? Who is the tree that turns into a stump that turns into an animal? We'll see if you're right.

Well, that was the dream. Neb told Daniel the dream. He asked, "Daniel, what does it mean?" Daniel told him, "King, this huge tree is you. [Yes, you guessed right!] You're so big that everybody in the world knows who you are. You're so powerful that you are like the tree. You provide shade for the animals because you are so big that you provide peace on the earth. You provide food for people. You're the biggest, most powerful person alive. But—are you living for God anymore? Are you worshipping God as the one true King? No, you're not! Therefore, God's going to turn you into a stump, and you'll go crazy. You won't know what is real anymore.

"After seven years, you'll get to grow back up into a tree again. You'll get to be king again. But for seven years you will think you're an animal. This will happen so you will remember that God's the one true King, and he gives kingdoms to whomever he wants."

Do you ever talk to yourself? Something like, "I wonder where this Lego piece should go?" Does your dad talk to himself? [Sorry!]

About a year later, Neb was in his palace talking to himself. He said, "Look at this great palace I built. I built this city by my power. And I built it for my honor." Did he build it all by his own power? No! Who gave Neb his brain, his strength, and his kingdom? Who is really King? [God.] To whom does God give kingdoms? [He gives them to whomever he wants.] So, why is Neb king? He's a king only because God gave the kingdom to him. Why does Neb think he's king? He thinks he is king because he's so great.

While Neb was saying these things to himself, a voice spoke to him. Maybe it was the voice of Jesus, or Gabriel, or Michael. The voice said, "The kingdom is gone from you. We're going to drive you away from people, and you're going to live with the beasts of the field.

You're going to eat grass like the ox for seven years until you know that God rules over people and gives the kingdom to whomever he wants." Immediately Neb went crazy.

Neb had to live alone out in the fields. He ate grass like a cow. He was wet in the mornings from sleeping outside. His hair grew long like a bird's feathers, and his nails grew out like bird claws. Why did he go crazy? So the world would know that God rules.

> What do you think Neb did when his seven crazy years were over?

What would it be like if all of a sudden you woke up from being crazy like King Neb? It might seem as if you've had a bad dream. You remember sniffing the walls and walking around on all fours. You remember living outside and people making fun of you. You remember it raining on you. You remember the hot days when you didn't know enough to come inside. The bad news is—it wasn't a dream! How would you feel after being out in the field for seven years? Your hair is long and tangled. Your toenails and fingernails look like claws because you didn't know enough to trim them. You've been going without clothes, and you smell bad. You smell thoroughly, completely, totally bad! You haven't had a bath in seven years, except when you walked through a pond. Now, all of a sudden, God gives you your mind back. You realize you used to be a king. But here you are walking on all fours, and you're naked out on the grass with the cows. What are you going to do?

The Bible says that at the end of seven years Neb cleaned himself up and said, "God's rule is forever. His kingdom continues for all time. . . . God does what he wants with the powers of heaven and the people on earth!" (Dan. 4:34–35 ICB).

Remember: You've Got His Word on It

Do you know the laws of the universe and how God rules the earth? Job 38:33

God reigns above the nations, sitting on his holy throne. Psalm 47:8

Then it will be known to the ends of the earth that God rules over Jacob. Psalm 59:13 NIV

"Don't be frightened, Mary," the angel told her, "for God has decided to bless you! You will become pregnant and have a son, and you are to name him Jesus. He will be very great and will be called the Son of the Most High. And the Lord God will give him the throne of his ancestor David. And he will reign over Israel forever; his Kingdom will never end!" Luke 1:30–33

17

A Hand without a Body

Scripture Passage: Daniel 5

So What? Give God honor!

For Parents: [Anything in brackets]

Do you remember our last story about King Neb? Why did he go crazy? What did he learn?

Neb had a grandson named Belshazzar. Poor kid; I wonder what they called him in school! We'll call him Bel. Neb was getting older, so Bel was running the country of Babylon. Bel knew all about what had happened to Neb when he went crazy, but Bel didn't believe in the one true God. Bel was spoiled and proud. He refused to honor God. He had over fifty temples in Babylon dedicated to false gods. [Your Bible may say that Belshazzar was Nebuchadnezzar's son. The term also means "descendant," just as Jesus is the son of David, the son of Abraham. History indicates that Belshazzar was probably his grandson.]

Describe your perfect birthday party. Whom would you invite? What would you do?

Bel decided to have a party. He didn't want a regular party. Bel was king, and he wanted a massive super-party! We're talking 1,000 friends! Yes, you heard right—he invited 1,000 friends to his party! The bad thing is that it wasn't a good kind of party.

This party was a real mess. While everyone was drinking wine, Bel gave orders to do something bad. This wasn't just a little bad; it was terribly bad. Years before, King Neb had taken a bunch of gold and silver goblets out of God's temple in Israel. He brought the goblets back to Babylon. Bel had seen the beautiful goblets and decided that he would make fun of God with them. He decided they would use the goblets to praise false gods! These goblets, made to worship God, were now going to be part of his bad party. Bel was not just dishonoring God—he was making fun of God!

What do you think God thought about what Bel was doing? Is it okay to get mad sometimes? When is it bad? When might it be okay? [Explain anger for selfish reasons versus anger for righteous reasons. Some-times anger is unavoidable, but how we handle it is our choice.]

God gets angry. In the Bible, God calls it righteous anger. That means getting mad for the right reason. Psalm 103:8 says that "God is slow to anger," but that means he can get angry. Bel was about to learn that making God angry isn't a good idea!

Suddenly, with all 1,000 people being rowdy in this huge banquet room, a hand showed up on the wall. This hand had no arm, no elbow, and no body. Wouldn't it be weird to see a hand kind of walking on the wall? The Bible says the fingers of the hand appeared. Maybe just the fingers were there. Oooh. That would be even weirder. The fingers probably engraved the plaster of the wall. Bel saw the hand write on the wall without a pen and without a body!

Near the lampstand in the royal palace, the king watched the hand as it wrote on the wall. What do you think the king was thinking? Maybe he was thinking he could take his sword and try to kill the hand. But, how do you kill a hand? The king's face turned white, and he was so frightened that his knees knocked and his legs gave way. Show me what happened when his legs gave way. What do you think he looked like? He wasn't making fun of God anymore!

Who is the smartest person you know? Do you think Bel was very smart?

The hand wrote four words on the wall. They were, "numbered, numbered, weighed, and split up." [The actual words in Aramaic were Mene, Mene, Tekel, Upharsin.] Now Bel was smart enough to know the hand that wrote on the wall was the hand of God. He wasn't smart enough to know what the four words meant, however. In fact, he went through all the wise men in his palace, and none of them could tell him what the words meant. He knew he was in big trouble with God, but he had no idea how much trouble until someone could tell him what the writing meant.

Finally, the queen came into the party room. She remembered that the prophet Daniel had helped King Neb. Daniel honored God. But, was Daniel still alive? Would he know what the writing meant?

If he knew, would he tell Bel? Immediately Bel sent for Daniel, the prophet of the one true God.

What do you think Daniel thought of Bel? Would you be scared to go before the king?

Daniel was brought in front of the king. Daniel might have been scared, because the king could kill him if he wanted. Scared or not, Daniel still spoke the truth. Here's what he said: "O king. You're having this big party, and you're using stuff from the temple. You're all proud, and you think you're big. But—you need to know that you haven't humbled yourself like King Nebuchadnezzar did." What does humble mean? It means to see yourself as God sees you. But Bel wasn't humble. He did not honor God, because he thought he was equal to God.

Daniel goes on to tell the king, "Here's what the words mean. They mean God has numbered your days and ended your kingdom. He has weighed your kingdom and found it wanting. That means you don't measure up; you're not living right. God warned you, and now the Medes and Persians will take over and divide your kingdom."

That very night Darius the Mede attacked Babylon and took over the kingdom. Bel, king of Babylon, died defending his city. That was the end of the kingdom of Babylon, because the king and his people didn't honor God.

Remember: You've Got His Word on It

Why do you think God wrote with just the hand? What does it mean to "honor" God? How did Daniel honor God? How can we honor him? We can honor God by . . .

Flying banners—May we shout for joy when we hear of your victory, flying banners to honor our God. May the LORD answer all your prayers. Psalm 20:5

Asking for forgiveness—Help us, O God of our salvation! Help us for the honor of your name. Oh, save us and forgive our sins for the sake of your name. Psalm 79:9

Taking care of your bodies—God bought you with a high price. So you must honor God with your body. 1 Corinthians 6:20

Showing kindness—Then the way you live will always honor and please the Lord, and you will continually do good, kind things for others. All the while, you will learn to know God better and better. Colossians 1:10

Staying faithful—So if your faith remains strong after being tried by fiery trials, it will bring you much praise and glory and honor on the day when Jesus Christ is revealed to the whole world. 1 Peter 1:7

Being good examples—Be careful how you live among your unbelieving neighbors. Even if they accuse you of doing wrong, they will see your honorable behavior, and they will believe and give honor to God when he comes to judge the world. 1 Peter 2:12

Worshipping him—Glory and honor to God forever and ever. He is the eternal King, the unseen one who never dies; he alone is God. Amen. 1 Timothy 1:17

— 18 —
Angel in Jail

Scripture Passage: Daniel 10

So What? Keep on praying; it's war out there!

For Parents: [Anything in brackets]

> Why do you think we have dreams? What's the scariest dream you've ever had? What's the best [fun, exciting, good] dream you have ever had?

Our last story was about a man named Daniel. This story is about something that happens a little later in his life. Daniel had a dream. This was a special dream, kind of like the dream that King Neb had a few chapters ago.

Occasionally God gives someone a special dream. It is not a normal, every-night kind of dream. It is an extra-special, had-to-come-from-God kind of dream. This was one of those. Somehow, Daniel knew that God was talking to him. Daniel was a special man, and this was a special dream.

Do you think God answers your prayers? What prayers has God answered for you? Has he ever answered, "No"? Has he ever answered, "Wait"?

Daniel didn't understand what his dream meant. So he prayed. When Daniel prayed for the answer to Neb's dream, God told him what it meant. When Daniel prayed for the answer to the hand's writing on the wall, God told him what it meant. When Daniel prayed this time for the answer to his own dream, God didn't tell him what it meant. Nothing. Nada. Zippo. No answer. Silence.

So Daniel prayed some more, and more, and more. Then he did something to make sure he wouldn't forget to pray each day. He fasted. Fasting is when you go without a certain kind of food [possibly all food] for a while. So every time you want that food you pray instead. It would be like going without chocolate. Every time you wanted a chocolate snack that would remind you to pray.

So, Daniel went without his favorite foods and prayed every time he wanted to eat them. He prayed and fasted and prayed. He did this for three weeks. He continued to pray. He continued to fast. Then came the day he received his answer.

Have you ever seen an angel? What do you think they look like? What do you think they do all day?

Twenty-four days after Daniel first prayed, an angel came in answer to his prayer. This is what the angel looked like:

He was dressed in bright white clothes.

He had a wide belt made out of gold, like a fancy gold watch-band around his waist.

His body was like a beautiful shiny stone you can see through.

His face was like trying to look at a flash of lightning.

His eyes were like looking into a fire.

His arms and legs were like polished brass.

His voice sounded like 1,000 people saying the same thing at the same time!

How would you feel if you were playing outside and all of a sudden a man like this showed up from nowhere? His face was like looking at the sun. You couldn't even look at his eyes without your eyes burning. His arms and legs looked like bright brass, and even his white clothes glowed. And when he talked, it sounded like a whole bunch of people talking at once. How do you think you would feel? Daniel wasn't in the presence of God, but he wasn't in the presence of a human either.

Daniel had had dreams from God before. Daniel had seen angels before. But this was too much for even him. The color left Daniel's face, and he turned white! He was so scared he couldn't move. Finally, he was able to get up, but he couldn't stop shaking. Can you show me what Daniel might have looked like?

> Have you ever been late for something important? What happened?

The first thing the angel told Daniel was, "Don't be afraid!" That's the same thing the angels told the shepherds the night Jesus was born. Angels have to say that to us humans a lot. When you think of how weird and powerful angels can look, you understand.

Then the angel told Daniel why he was late. What do you think his excuse was? Did he say God had forgotten Daniel's prayer? Was the angel lazy? No, he was held hostage for three weeks!

After Daniel had prayed, the angel left heaven and came to bring Daniel the answer to his prayer. Then some messenger of Satan held the angel hostage for three weeks! We don't know how he did this. Somehow, the demon was more powerful than that angel was. We don't know if he held him captive, like in a jail, or if he was fighting him for that long. At any rate, the angel couldn't get to Daniel. So Daniel kept praying, and the angel kept trying to come.

Have you ever been stuck where you needed help? Who rescued you?

Daniel, probably the greatest man of God on the planet, needed help. And, this super-powerful angel needed help. So what did God do? He sent Michael, one of the generals of the angelic army in heaven and probably the most powerful of all. When Michael got down to the fight or the jail, it was all over. The demon wasn't going to mess with Michael! Now the angel could go to Daniel, and Daniel had his prayer answered. The angel explained the dream to Daniel. What was the dream? Sorry, that's for our next book!

Talking to God is important business, and he always answers our prayers. Not many people ever get to see an angel, but that doesn't mean angels aren't out there. God put this story in the Bible to remind us how important it is to keep praying. Don't give up; he will answer.

God wants you to be a powerful prayer warrior like Daniel. God can always send powerful angels in answer to your prayers.

He has even more powerful angels than those Daniel saw, like Michael.

God is the most powerful being of all, and when we need him, he's always there. He sent his Son to die for us; he lives in us if we believe in him, and he will come back for us.

Don't fear; keep praying. He will answer; nothing can stop him!

Remember: You've Got His Word on It

So, friends, we can now—without hesitation—walk right up to God, into "the Holy Place." Jesus has cleared the way by the blood of his sacrifice, acting as our priest before God. The "curtain" into God's presence is his body. So let's *do* it—full of belief, confident that we're presentable inside and out. Let's keep a firm grip on the promises that keep us going. He always keeps his word. Hebrews 10:19–23 MESSAGE

19

The Underwater City

Scripture Passage: Ezekiel 26

So What? You can trust God!

For Parents: [Anything in brackets]

> Would you like to know the future? Would you like to know what you will get for Christmas or what you will be when you grow up?

God can be trusted. He knows the future, and what he says will happen *will* happen. He proves this in Ezekiel 26. Five hundred eighty-six years before Jesus was born, God spoke through the prophet Ezekiel. God told Ezekiel what the future was going to be for a city called Tyre. It's pronounced like a tire on your car, but spelled T-Y-R-E.

If someone asked you to tell the future, what could you say about tomorrow that will probably come true? [Have your children think of simple things, such as, the sun will come up; it will snow somewhere in Canada.] What would be a harder prediction? [Anything specific or out of the ordinary, such as, kindergarteners will learn calculus; Phoenix will have a blizzard.]

Some people today talk about being able to predict the future, but they don't do it the same way God does. God gives specific, detailed predictions. That's why he can be trusted—he's accurate, right down to the smallest detail.

The future of Tyre wasn't a pleasant story. Tyre was an extremely wicked city. Destruction was coming. What happened to Tyre is different from any other city in history. Here is what God said would happen:

Many nations will come against Tyre.

The walls around the city will be destroyed.

The towers around the walls will be torn down.

The ruins of the city (stones and stuff the homes are made from) will be scraped away.

The city will look bald, like a bare rock.

People will go fishing (spread their nets) over the city. (So, somehow, it must become an underwater city!)

That was God's prophecy. It seems both weird and impossible. Of course, lots of cities get destroyed. It would be easy to say, "I'm a prophet, and I say that someday [your city] will be destroyed." Well, probably someday it will. Nothing lasts forever, not even cities. But to say that [your city] would be scraped bare like a rock and the walls and towers would be knocked down and you will go fishing on top of it, that would be pretty weird! Not only that, it would be impossible to make happen.

> What would have to happen to [your city] for it to look like the top of a rock? What would have to happen to [your city] for people to go fishing on top of it?

Several different nations attacked Tyre over many years. One of the first armies to come against Tyre was Babylon, back when Nebuchadnezzar was king. Do you remember King Neb? He came against Tyre and tore down the walls and the towers. It took him thirteen years to conquer Tyre.

[Although the prophecy is in the Bible, the fulfillment of it comes from our study of history. Many wonderful fulfillments of Bible prophecy like this one can be found in Josh McDowell's *The New Evidence That Demands a Verdict*. It's a great resource, but don't read it if you want to stay awake late at night. It's a resource book, not a story book. The information included here is just hitting the highlights of what Josh includes of Tyre's history.]

Three hundred years later a person called Alexander the Great came along. He wanted to take over the world. He conquered one country, another country, then another. He was coming close to Tyre. The people in Tyre were scared because they were in Alexander's way. Do you know what they did? About a half mile away from Tyre was

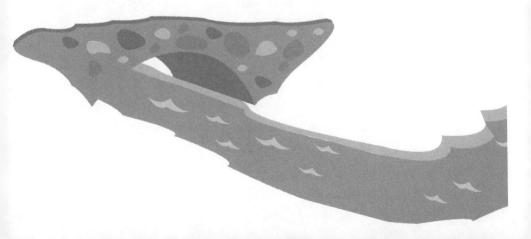

an island. When the people saw Alexander coming, they went to the island and built new houses out there. They brought all their stuff to the island. They brought their toys, their dogs and cats; they even brought their little brothers! They used an army of boats to bring the entire city onto the island. When Alexander came to take over Tyre, what was there? Nothing of value! All their houses were there, but they were completely empty!

It was as if we had built another house out on an island and moved out there. This house would be empty; we would be living on the island.

Now what did Alexander want to do? He wanted to take over the world. Of course, he was upset that he couldn't take over Tyre. He didn't have a navy. He had no boats. The people sitting out there on the island must have laughed at Alexander.

Have you ever put a bunch of stones in the water so you could walk across the water? Have you ever walked across a creek by jumping from stone to stone? Did you fall in?

Alexander didn't like being laughed at, not one bit. He decided he would make a bridge to the island. Can you guess what material he used for the bridge? He made it out of the city! He had his army start tearing down all the empty houses. They were stone and brick houses, perfect material for a land bridge. The army threw the bricks and stones into the water. They tore the whole city down. Every house, every wall was gone. They still hadn't quite made it to the island, so they started sweeping the city and throwing the dust into the water! So the old city of Tyre looked like the . . . top . . . of . . . the . . . rock. It was totally bare—no houses, no trees, no walls, no stone streets—nothing was left. Alexander's army took everything out, and the people of Tyre weren't laughing anymore.

Finally, the army walked across all those old houses and over to the island. Then they took over the city that was on the island as well.

So where is the old city of Tyre now? How did Alexander's army make the bridge? How long would it last? What do you think happened to the bridge?

So where was the old city now? It was the bridge to the island. Alexander's army didn't build the bridge to last long. They only needed to use it for one trip. Remember, they made it by throwing a bunch of debris into the water so they could walk over the top of it. Over the years, the water washed the bridge down. So now the old city of Tyre is underwater, and people go fishing on top of the old Tyre. They catch the fish that love hiding in the stones of the old city. Then they spread their nets where Tyre was, because it is now "bare as a rock"; it's a good place to let the nets dry out as they clean the fish. So, the old city looks like the top of the rock, and it's underwater.

The people of Tyre didn't trust God. No one believed Tyre could become a rock and an underwater city, so they didn't change. Nevertheless, everything came true, just like God said. Do you know why it happened just as he said it would? It's because he's all truth. It was as if he had already been there and seen it. For God, your birthday next year has already happened. He's already seen it!

So, when God promises to forgive your sins if you believe in Jesus, you can trust him to do just that. When he promises to be with you always, you can trust that he will never leave you alone. When he promises to return for you, you know that he's coming back!

Remember: You've Got His Word on It

O God, I praise your word. I trust in God, so why should I be afraid? What can mere mortals do to me? Psalm 56:4

O my people, trust in him at all times. Pour out your heart to him, for God is our refuge. Psalm 62:8

See, God has come to save me. I will trust in him and not be afraid. The LORD GOD is my strength and my song; he has become my salvation. Isaiah 12:2

Trust in the LORD always, for the LORD GOD is the eternal Rock. Isaiah 26:4

We know how much God loves us, and we have put our trust in him. God is love, and all who live in love live in God, and God lives in them. 1 John 4:16

20

When Bones Walk

Scripture Passage: Ezekiel 37

So What? Miracles still happen!

For Parents: [Anything in brackets. A map or globe with Israel on it would be helpful.]

> Some people in the Bible have visions—do you remember what a vision is? A vision is when God takes you somewhere to see something. It's like a dream.

Ezekiel was a pastor 570 years before Jesus was born. In Ezekiel 37, we read about a vision in which God the Holy Spirit took Ezekiel to a valley that was full of bones. The bones were everywhere. These were not alligator bones or dog bones or guinea pig bones. These were human bones. What kind of human bones do you think Ezekiel saw? He saw skulls and leg bones and arm bones. It wasn't yucky, and there was no blood, because these were old bones.

The Holy Spirit and Ezekiel walked through the old bones, which were scattered all over the valley. The bones were white and dry because they were extremely old.

> God asked Ezekiel a simple question: "Can these bones live again?" What's the answer?

Ezekiel knew the bones were not alive. He also knew God could do anything. So Ezekiel answered: "Well, God, only you know if they can live." Then God said he was going to make the old, scattered, dried-out bones come back to life! He said he would make them come back together; then would put skin on them and make them live again! Would you want to see that?

Well, Ezekiel had no choice. He was standing in the valley when he heard a rustling noise. It got louder. The bones were moving! Arm bones connected to shoulder bones. Skulls connected to spines. Toes connected to feet. What a weird dream! Would you be scared by now?

Listen to what Ezekiel says happened next. God is talking to him and says:

Speak to these bones and say, "Dry bones, listen to the word of the LORD! This is what the Sovereign

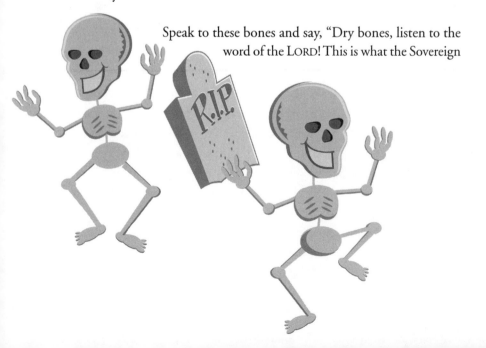

LORD says: Look! I am going to breathe into you and make you live again! I will put flesh and muscles on you and cover you with skin. I will put breath into you, and you will come to life. Then you will know that I am the LORD."

So I spoke these words, just as he told me. Suddenly as I spoke, there was a rattling noise all across the valley. The bones of each body came together and attached themselves as they had been before.

Ezekiel 37:4–7

Ezekiel could do nothing but watch. Once the bones came together, there were skeletons standing all around him, but they weren't alive. Then he saw muscles and skin connect to the bones. But the people were still not alive.

Then God told Ezekiel to "Speak to the winds and say: 'This is what the Sovereign LORD says: Come, O breath, from the four winds! Breathe into these dead bodies so that they may live again.'" So I spoke as he commanded me, and the wind entered the bodies, and they began to breathe. They all came to life and stood up on their feet—a great army of them (vv. 9–10).

A huge army surrounded Ezekiel. Now they were alive; the bones had come to life!

God showed Ezekiel this vision as a picture of something that would happen in the future. Sometimes we use pictures too. Maybe your dad looks at a lightbulb and says, "I bet that's how the back of my head will look in a few years!" God was giving Ezekiel a picture of what he was going to do for the people of Israel.

> Do you like seeing pictures of places you've never been? Of animals you've never seen? Why?

The nation of Israel was without hope. Israel had lost her last war, and the nation was in ruins. It happened long ago, so they felt like a bunch of old bones. Other nations had come in and conquered them. When they were conquered, they became prisoners and had to leave Israel. The invading armies forced them to live in other lands. They felt old. They weren't a country anymore; they were scattered all around the world. The stories of King David and Solomon were a distant memory. The nation of Israel was a bunch of old bones.

However, God said he would make those old bones come back to life. That meant he would make Israel come back to life! How could God do this? When would God do this? How long would his people have to wait?

Five hundred years after Ezekiel died, Jesus lived in Israel, but Israel wasn't a nation yet. They weren't free; Rome ruled them. So, five hundred years later they were still like old bones. There was no life. One thousand years later—no Israel. Two thousand years later—still no Israel. Twenty-five hundred years later, there was . . . Israel!

In 1948, Israel became a nation again! It was 2,500 years after Ezekiel had his vision when God finally did what he said he would do. Good grief—2,500 years! Why did God wait so long? The longer God waited, the more impossible it was that Israel could become a nation again. That is precisely why he waited. No other nation has ceased to exist for 2,500 years and then come back to life. Rome didn't do it. Greece didn't do it. Russia and America didn't do it. Only Israel did it. That miracle happened only about fifty-five years ago. They became a nation because God put them back together. Just as those old bones couldn't come back together without help, Israel couldn't come back together on its own. God was doing something!

Does God still do miracles? Do you know of any?

Today God is still bringing Jewish people back to Israel. The Jewish people of Israel were scattered all over the world, like the bones in the valley. They were in the Ukraine, the United States, Europe, Russia, Canada, etc. [Show on map.] People choosing to go back to Israel are like the bones coming back together. Then the people became a nation again. That's like the skin coming back on the bones. [If you have a map or globe with Israel on it, you could show it now.] When you see Israel on the map, you are looking at a miracle. Some of these people are now giving their lives to Jesus. That's when they become alive again. That's another miracle, and it happens every day!

Remember: You've Got His Word on It

What other nation on earth is like Israel? What other nation, O God, have you redeemed from slavery to be your own people? You made a great name for yourself when you rescued your people from Egypt. You performed awesome miracles and drove out the nations and gods that stood in their way. 2 Samuel 7:23

For he does great works too marvelous to understand. He performs miracles without number. Job 5:9

O LORD my God, you have done many miracles for us. Your plans for us are too numerous to list. If I tried to recite all your wonderful deeds, I would never come to the end of them. Psalm 40:5

For you are great and perform great miracles. You alone are God. Psalm 86:10

Let us see your miracles again; let our children see your glory at work. Psalm 90:16

21

When Pigs Fly

Scripture Passage: Matthew 8:28–34

So What? Sometimes I get scared, but even then I am safe!

For Parents: [Anything in brackets]

> Can you name any animals that fly? Do you know of any rodents that can fly? [Flying squirrels were all we could think of.]

This is a story with pigs in it. It's a very short story—only seven verses long in the Bible. Jesus and his disciples crossed a large lake, and a big surprise hit them when they arrived at the other side.

> What are tombs? Where do we put dead bodies now? Are graveyards scary to you?

When Jesus and his disciples arrived at the other side of the lake, two men came to him. These weren't ordinary men; these were men with demons in them! They lived in the caves on the side of the lake, where dead people were buried. They were dangerous men. So dangerous the people couldn't use the roads by the caves anymore, for fear of what the men might do to them.

The two men ran to Jesus out of their home, a graveyard. [Have you ever seen the movie *My Dog Skip?* The boy in that movie had to spend a night in the graveyard. These men had to live in the graveyard.] Think how scary it would be to have two grown men run to you out of a graveyard!

What does it mean to be demon possessed?

The Bible says these two men were demon possessed. That means they had demons controlling them. Demons are angels that chose to follow Satan long ago.

These men did horrible, wicked things. They were living outside, doing whatever the demons wanted them to do. They were violent. What does the word *violent* mean? It means "evil" and "aggressive." They would smash and break things. They were so aggressive that no one would even use the roads close to them. No one wanted to go near that graveyard. These two men were powerful because of the demons controlling them. We often become afraid of what is more powerful than we are. We're afraid of things we don't understand. Was Jesus afraid? Of course not; he understood them. Did Jesus go down those roads? Sure; he was more powerful than a couple demons. Did Jesus go right into a graveyard that had two violent, aggressive, mean, demon-possessed men living in it? Yup; he went there, and he went there on purpose!

Do you think Jesus was scared? What if you were one of Jesus' disciples and it was your first week on the job, would you be scared? [I think I would kind of stand back so the other eleven and Jesus could go first!]

Jesus went there. The two men started screaming when he came close. "What do you want to do with us, Son of God?" they shouted. "Did you come to torture us?"

Who is really speaking? Is it the men or the demons inside them? It's the demons talking through the men. Do you think Jesus was scared? No way! You're only afraid of what's more powerful than you are. However, the disciples were terrified. In fact, they probably stayed behind by the boat where they could paddle away if they needed to!

Do you think anything scares Satan? Does anything scare his demons?

Some distance from Jesus and the two men were some other people with a large herd of pigs. They probably didn't like getting too close to the tombs and the possessed men, so they stayed back on some other roads. We read in Mark 5:13 that the people had about 2,000 pigs. The demons started begging Jesus, "If you're going to drive us out, send us into the pigs!"

Why were the demons so scared? It's because they were dealing with Jesus. Jesus was God with skin on, and God is so powerful that he terrifies demons. The demons knew Jesus could do whatever he wanted. He could send the demons to hell or to nowhere at all. Jesus thought that sending them into the pigs was a good idea, so he said to the demons, "Go!" [At the time of Christ, before the cross, believers were to keep the Old Testament dietary laws. God had told the people not to eat pork, a law that didn't change until after Pentecost, in the Book of Acts. These men were making money raising pigs for consumption, in direct violation of God's command.] Immediately the demons came out of the two men and went into the pigs. That made the whole herd of pigs demon possessed. How many demons do you think were living in those two men? It must have been a lot. Two thousand possessed pigs means there were at least 2,000 demons! [That is because demons can be in only one place at a time. Only God can be in more than one place at a time. Only God is omnipresent.] That makes 1,000 demons in each person! Whoa! That would be a lot of bad in each guy!

> **What can fly farther, a squirrel or a pig? What happens to pigs that try to fly?**

At the command of Jesus, the demons came out of the men and went into the 2,000 pigs. The whole herd of pigs went crazy. They ran over a steep bank (like over the cliff). And they flew! Where did they fly? Well, even demons can't make pigs fly too far. The Bible says they flew into the lake and drowned.

The two men immediately changed into their right minds. They were normal again. The herdsmen, who had been watching over the pigs, went into town and told the townspeople what Jesus had done for the demon-possessed men. They

told the townspeople what Jesus had done with the demons and to the pigs. Then the townspeople came to meet Jesus. What do you think they asked Jesus? Did they ask him to heal their diseases or to forgive their sins? Did they thank him for healing the two troubled men?

No. They asked him to leave. They were scared of Jesus because they knew he was more powerful than they were. Before Jesus came, things in the town were pretty normal. Two crazy men were living in the graveyard, but the townspeople didn't really care; they could avoid the graveyard, no big deal. The people had their pigs on the hillside; they could eat pork, no big deal. But when Jesus came, everything changed. The crazy men became normal. The pigs flew into the lake and died. Now everything was changing. Jesus always wants to change things, but the townspeople didn't want to change. They were afraid of change, so they were afraid of Jesus. They kicked Jesus out of town and said, "We want to keep things as they are."

What is scary? [Things more powerful than we are; things outside of our control.]

There is no life scarier but safer than a life given to Jesus. He helps us to change every day, and that can be scary. He is more powerful than anyone else is. We don't control our lives; he does. Put your life in the hands of Jesus, and you will have nothing to fear. In this story, no one was safer or more scared than the disciples were. Follow Jesus, and you'll always be safe.

Remember: You've Got His Word on It

Trust in the LORD and do good. Then you will live safely in the land and prosper. Psalm 37:3

The name of the LORD is a strong fortress; the godly run to him and are safe. Proverbs 18:10

Fearing people is a dangerous trap, but to trust the LORD means safety. Proverbs 29:25

The Roman officer and the other soldiers at the crucifixion were terrified by the earthquake and all that had happened. They said, "Truly, this was the Son of God!" Matthew 27:54

And they were filled with awe and said among themselves, "Who is this man, that even the wind and waves obey him?" Mark 4:41

They were all terrified when they saw him. But Jesus spoke to them at once. "It's all right," he said. "I am here! Don't be afraid." Mark 6:50

22

The Grave Robber

Scripture Passage: Matthew 27

So What? Get in line; you have a number!

For Parents: [Anything in brackets]

Have you ever had to wait in line with a number? Have you ever waited with your parents for a seat in a restaurant? What's good about having a number?

There's a wonderful, huge, fun party mentioned in the Bible called the "Feast of Firstfruits." [Read more about this feast in Leviticus 23: 9–14.] It comes just once a year, in the springtime. The Bible calls it a feast because there was always lots of food at this party and "firstfruits" because the farmers would bring the first part of their crops to the Lord in Jerusalem. It's kind of like bringing the first of our money to him on Sundays. We still have this party each year, but now we call it another name. We call it Easter. Easter is a name people made up, but the Bible name for Easter is the Feast of Firstfruits.

Thousands of people came to Jerusalem every year for this huge party. The day Jesus rose from the dead was on the Feast of Firstfruits, so we know many people were in Jerusalem that day. You probably remember the Easter story. Wicked people had Jesus crucified, and his friends buried him in a cave. On Easter Sunday, what the Bible calls the Feast of Firstfruits, Jesus rose from the dead. But that's not the only important thing that happened that day. Something weird happened!

Do you know what else happened that day? Do you have any guesses? One more clue: It is something that might sound scary. Did that help?

On the day Jesus rose from the dead, he did something that seems scary when we first hear about it. Are you ready? Sure? Maybe we should just stop here. . . . Well, he brought people back to life from the dead! He gave them new bodies and brought them back to town with him! Can you imagine what happened when people saw their friends and relatives who had died walking around town? What a shock it would be! It sounds weird, but wouldn't it be great to have [a loving Christian relative or friend who has died] come back and tell you how wonderful life is living with Jesus? He [or she] could tell you about how fun and exciting life has been for him since he died. It would be terrific fun once we weren't afraid anymore. We could talk about the good times we used to have, and we could tell him what has happened since he died. He could tell us what living in heaven with Jesus is like. We could celebrate his 125th birthday party!

Do you remember what the farmers did on the Feast of Firstfruits? Right; they brought the first of their crops to God in Jerusalem. However, Jesus was not a farmer. What would he bring to God in Jerusalem? Farmers put seeds in the ground in order to see new crops come up. Jesus washes our sins away in order to see a new life come up. So, instead of bringing crops to Jerusalem, Jesus brought people to Jerusalem. Farmers brought their new crops. The crops were born, brought back to life, from a dead seed. Jesus brought these people back to life from the dead! Matthew 27:52–53 says: "The tombs broke open and the bodies of many holy people who had died were raised to life. They came out of the tombs, and after Jesus' resurrection they went into the holy city and appeared to many people" (NIV).

What do you think happened when these people came back to town? What would you do?

When we wait in line, we call it "waiting our turn." We know that if we have a number and are waiting, sometime soon someone will call our number. The Bible calls Jesus "the firstfruits." That means he's the one person who gets to have the number "1." On Easter he became the number one person to rise from the dead, never to die again. Then he brought others back from the dead too. They were numbers 2, 3, 4, maybe up to 100 or so. If you know Jesus as your Savior, you have a number also. God gave you this number, and only he knows what it is. First Corinthians 15:22–23 says, "in Christ all will be made alive. But each in his own turn: Christ, the firstfruits; then, when he comes, those who belong to him" (NIV). So, when Jesus comes back for us, he will call each of us in order. If you believe in Jesus, he has your number. So get in line—sometime soon he will call it!

Remember: You've Got His Word on It

What will it be like when Jesus comes back for us? Are you ready for him to come? We don't know when Jesus is going to come back for us. We do know some things about what will happen when he comes. We know that:

1 Corinthians 1:7–9

He wants us to look forward to it.
We will be free from all blame.
He is coming as your friend.
He is coming for you.
He always does what he says.

1 Corinthians 15:35–52

We will receive new bodies that never die, as Jesus has now.
He will come so fast it will be like a blink of your eye.
You will hear a trumpet when he comes (kind of like ringing the doorbell to let you know he is here!).

1 Thessalonians 4:13–18

He will bring Michael, the archangel, with him.
He will bring all those who have died before and believe in Jesus with him.
He will come for only those who believe that Jesus died for their sins and rose again from the dead.
Those who trust in Jesus will live with him from then on.

23

Caught in a Lie

Scripture Passage: Acts 5:1–11

So What? It never pays to lie to God!

For Parents: [Anything in brackets]

Is there a good day to lie? Do some lies get you in more trouble than others? Can you give me an example when you didn't get into trouble at all for telling a lie? Can you give me an example when you got into lots of trouble?

Some days you may tell a lie and feel like you got away with it. Of course, you didn't get away with it. God knows you lied, and so do you. That's why you feel guilty inside.

Let me tell you about a couple of people who lied to God. This story takes place right after Jesus lived, died on the cross for you, and rose again. Jesus went to heaven, and the church was growing. In just a few short weeks, the church had grown from a few disciples to over

15,000 people! [In Acts 4:4, Luke records about 5,000 men. If there is just one woman and child for each man, we have over 15,000 new believers in the church.]

The church was an exciting place to be. People were excited about God, and the church was growing. New people were joining every day, and God was doing fantastic miracles through the apostles. Now here come the liars.

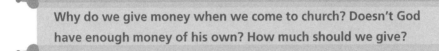

Why do we give money when we come to church? Doesn't God have enough money of his own? How much should we give?

There was a married couple coming to the church; Ananias was the husband, and Sapphira the wife. They sold some land they owned and decided to give the money to the church. Is that a good thing to do? Sure.

Let's pretend we're going to have a garage sale next weekend. You sell [pick a nice toy or belonging of the child] and are paid twenty dollars for it. You decide to give some of the money to the church. Is that a good thing to do? Sure it is.

When you give the money, you go up to the front so everyone can see what you're doing. You grab a microphone and speak into it so everyone will hear you. You say: "Hello out there! I want you all to know that I'm giving money to the church today." You hold five dollars high above your head. "I just sold my favorite [insert toy], and this is all the money I was paid for it. I am giving every penny of it to God's church here because I love him so much!"

Would that be a good thing to do? Of course not. It's lying. It's bragging and trying to impress people with a lie. It's trying to make them believe you're doing something you're not doing. That is exactly what Ananias and Sapphira did. They went in front of the church and said they were giving all the money from the sale of their land to the church. But that was a lie. They gave only *part* of the money.

Was it sin for Ananias and Sapphira to sell their land? Was it sin for them to keep part of the money? No, the land and money belonged to them. How did they sin? Why do you think they did this?

Ananias and Sapphira lied because they wanted the church people to like them. They wanted to be popular. They wanted people to say, "Wow, Ananias and Sapphira are so unselfish! Can you believe they gave *all* the money they received from selling their land to the church? They must be really close to God!" That's what they wanted to hear, but what they heard was awfully, horribly different.

Ananias came to church first. You can imagine him in front of the people, bragging about how he was giving all of his land money to God's work. Peter was also in front of the church, and Peter knew the truth. Peter, in front of everyone, started asking Ananias some questions. He asked, "Ananias, why are you letting Satan rule you and why are you lying to God the Holy Spirit?" How would you answer? Next, Peter asked, "Before you sold the land, didn't it belong to you?" How would you answer? Then Peter asked, "After you sold the land, couldn't you have spent the money any way you wanted?" How would you answer?

When Ananias heard Peter ask these questions, something horrible happened to him. Ananias fell down and died! Everyone who saw what happened was super scared. Just think if someone went in front of church and said, "I just sold this in a garage sale; here's every penny of the money." And the pastor got up and said, "Wait a minute. That's not all of the money." Then boom—the person fell down dead. Whoa.

Some men carried Ananias outside the church and buried his body. About three hours later, Sapphira came to the church. She didn't know what happened to her husband, so she told the exact same lie! They must have practiced what they were going to say so their lies would match.

Peter asked her, "Why did you agree to lie to God? Look! The men who buried your husband are here, and now they are going to bury you too!" At that moment, she fell to the floor dead, just as her husband did!

You've lied, but you didn't die. What do you think makes this lie different? Why did they die?

God is gracious, and although we deserve to die for our sins, we usually live a long time on the earth—even though all of us have sinned. Ananias and Sapphira did a number of things when they lied that forced God to act.

First, they were testing God to see how much they could get away with. [That's the idea of "testing the Spirit of the Lord" in verse 9.] Have you ever pushed your parents to see how bad you could be before they punished you? That's what Ananias and Sapphira were doing. If you keep pushing, sooner or later your parents have to act.

They were also lying in front of the entire church. If God didn't act and the truth of their lie came out later, then it would look like God was tricked. He couldn't be all-knowing because Ananias and Sapphira lied to God, right in front of the church, and God did nothing. No, God had to act to show the church he is all-knowing, and that he doesn't like sin, especially lying in his church.

Finally, because what they did was in front of people, they had to be disciplined in front of people. God used them as an example to help others in the church remember to do what is right. They lied to Peter, to the people in the church, and to the Holy Spirit who is God. That's not a very smart thing to do. It's not smart because we can never get away with it; he knows everything. And, it isn't smart because God takes lying to him very seriously. It's always better to tell the truth.

Remember: You've Got His Word on It

Teach me your ways, O LORD, that I may live according to your truth! Grant me purity of heart, that I may honor you. Psalm 86:11

Truth stands the test of time; lies are soon exposed. Proverbs 12:19

A wise person is hungry for truth, while the fool feeds on trash. Proverbs 15:14

Get the truth and don't ever sell it; also get wisdom, discipline, and discernment. Proverbs 23:23

For God is Spirit, so those who worship him must worship in spirit and in truth. . . . And you will know the truth, and the truth will set you free. . . . I am the way, the truth, and the life. No one can come to the Father except through me. John 4:24, 8:32, 14:6

I could have no greater joy than to hear that my children live in the truth. 3 John 1:4

24

Hungry Worms

Scripture Passage: Acts 12

So What? Every good gift comes from God!

For Parents: [Anything in brackets]

Do your parents punish you when you do wrong? How quickly do they act to punish you? Does God punish us for our sin also?

First, let's talk about the bad news. Everything dies. When I was a young boy living in Arizona I caught a desert tortoise. Mortise the Tortoise was the perfect name. He was so cool. He tunneled down into a hole in our backyard and stayed there most the time. When he came out I would bring him inside and feed him lettuce and whatever else looked good in my mom's fridge. One day we were going over to a friend's house across town. "Hey Mom," I asked, "can I bring Mortise with us?" "Sure, just make sure he doesn't get loose in the car." So I put Mortise in a big bucket and off we went.

We had a great time at our friend's house. It was so much fun I forgot all about Mortise. It wasn't until we arrived back home that I remembered Mortise was still in their backyard stuck in that bucket. By the time we called and had the family check on him it was too late. Mortise was dead. Death is bad news.

There was a time on the earth when everything didn't die. God made us to live forever. But then Eve sinned, and Adam sinned, and I sinned, and you sinned. God is perfect and has to punish sin. Romans 6:23 says, "The payment for sin is death" (GOD'S WORD). Since all of us have sinned, all of us have to die. That's bad news!

Now let's hear the good news. Romans 6:23 goes on to say, "the gift that God freely gives is everlasting life found in Christ Jesus our Lord" (GOD'S WORD). God doesn't immediately punish us for our sins. He could, but he doesn't. He gives us time to trust Jesus, who died on the cross for our sins. If we trust Jesus, we will live forever. Even after we die we will continue to live with God. We'll see his light and beauty. We'll continue to have his help and friendship. If we reject Jesus, we will never know God. We'll never see his light and beauty. We'll never know his help and friendship. That's why God doesn't punish us for our sins right away. He wants to give us time to believe in Jesus.

Sometimes, because God doesn't punish people right away, they refuse to believe he's real. They think, "Hey, I've gotten away with all my sins so far in life. God must be a fake. Maybe he's dead. Anyway, I'll just keep sinning, because nothing is stopping me. If God is real, he can stop me anytime."

Herod Get-a-Grip, otherwise known as Herod Agrippa, thought like that. He sinned a lot, and God didn't seem to do anything about it. Herod became worse, and God still didn't act. God was waiting for Herod to accept Jesus. Finally, Herod Get-a-Grip arrested the apostle Peter. God could have punished Herod for his sins then, but he didn't. Instead, God rescued Peter, but nothing happened to Herod. Then Herod murdered one of Jesus' and Peter's best friends, the apostle James! Would God act now? No, he wouldn't. God gave Herod another chance to get a grip and turn to Jesus. But Herod didn't turn.

What things bring you compliments? What does God help you to do? What things do you give God the credit for doing in your life?

Herod did some horrible things to Peter and James, and he did them for a reason. Herod wanted power. He wanted people to like him. There were people in Herod's kingdom who didn't like Peter, so Herod arrested Peter. They didn't like James, so Herod murdered James. This made the people like Herod. If they liked him more, he would have more power.

[The background information in the next few paragraphs comes from *The Bible Knowledge Commentary* and the *JFB Commentary*. If you don't have any Bible commentaries, these two are a great place to start. A more complete history of this time can be found in Josephus's *Antiquities of the Jews* 19.8.2.]

Herod Get-a-Grip had his 54th birthday coming up and he wanted to do something special. He decided to travel to the town of Caesarea. The people there really liked him. It would be a good place to celebrate. Herod had recently worked a deal with the people of Caesarea to make sure they had the food they needed for the winter. They liked that. They liked what he had done with Peter and James. Not only that, Caesarea was a special place to Get-a-Grip. His grandfather, Herod the Great, had built a huge auditorium in Caesarea. His grandpa made this auditorium so well that even today, 2,000 years later, the remains of it are still standing! Today you can go to Caesarea and see what part of it looks like. Herod Get-a-Grip loved to speak in his grandpa's auditorium back in Caesarea. He decided to go there for his birthday to speak to the people.

It's always a big deal when a president, king, queen, or prime minister comes to town. It was no different in Caesarea. The townspeople cleaned up the auditorium. They cleaned up the entire city. Everyone wanted to get tickets to see Get-a-Grip. King Herod was excited too. He shined his shoes. He shined his crown. He shined his teeth and even cleaned his ears! He put on his fanciest robe. The people brought his throne chair onto the stage for everyone to see.

The city decorated the auditorium for King Herod. The people began arriving; they came, and they kept coming. Finally, every seat was full; people were standing in the aisles, and more people were coming! The place was as full as a Christmas stocking. Then Herod arrived.

He walked in slowly, letting his robes flow behind him. The auditorium erupted with applause. The people loved him. He spoke, and they loved him more! The more he spoke, the more they clapped. The people saw the king in his shiny shoes with his shiny crown. They saw the royal throne and the flash of his white teeth. They were overwhelmed and began yelling, "He's a god, not a man! He's a god, not a man!"

Herod loved it. He loved all of it. He loved the decorations and his sparkling crown. He loved his huge throne and his squeaky-clean ears. Most of all, he loved being called a god. "Yes," he must have been thinking, "give me your worship! Worship me, Herod Get-a-Grip! I'm more than a man, I'm a god!"

In Herod's day people believed you could tell if a person was good or bad by how they died. How do you think they thought good people died? [They thought it would be quick and relatively painless. Good people died with their families, giving a blessing, etc.] How do you think they thought bad people died?

When Herod let the people call him a god, God said, "Herod, that's enough! Get a grip! It's bad enough you arrested my servant, Peter. It's awful that you murdered my friend James. Now, you're claiming to be God. That's too much. Herod, I waited as long as I could. I can't put off your punishment for sin any longer. You rejected Jesus for the last time. You're going to die."

God wanted the people of Caesarea to know Herod was just a man; he wasn't a god. Back when Herod lived, people thought the worst kind of death was dying from a stomach problem, or even worse, if you died from worms. Without refrigeration and freezers, people could get worms from bad meat. The worms could then kill you by eating you from the inside out. Yuck, what could be worse? That is precisely what happened to Herod. He died of both a stomach problem and a worm problem. The worms ate his stomach! The people immediately knew that Herod was a man, and a bad man, not a god. Herod died. He was separated from the people he loved and the God he had avoided.

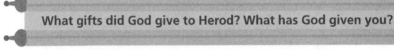

What gifts did God give to Herod? What has God given you?

God gave Herod a kingdom. He had money, a crown, and a throne. He had friends, power, and shiny shoes. What Herod didn't realize is that God gave all these gifts to him. Herod thought he had earned them all on his own. That's what it means to get a grip. Get a grip and understand there is no way we could have earned all we have on our own. We didn't earn our parents or our brains. We didn't earn our bodies, our talents, or our looks. Every good gift comes from God!

You have what you have because God gave it to you. God calls that his "grace." [Strong's Greek and Hebrew Dictionary defines grace (the Greek word *Charis*) as "gift, joy, benefit, or pleasure" among other words. A good definition for grace is "joy giving."] If you do well, it's not because you're smart and strong. It's because God has given you a good body, good food, and a good brain. We need to thank God for what we have instead of taking the glory ourselves. Let's get a grip!

Remember: You've Got His Word on It

Children are a gift from the LORD; they are a reward from him. Psalm 127:3

To enjoy your work and accept your lot in life—that is indeed a gift from God. Ecclesiastes 5:19

I am leaving you with a gift—peace of mind and heart. And the peace I give isn't like the peace the world gives. So don't be troubled or afraid. John 14:27

Each of you must turn from your sins and turn to God, and be baptized in the name of Jesus Christ for the forgiveness of your sins. Then you will receive the gift of the Holy Spirit. Acts 2:38

A spiritual gift is given to each of us as a means of helping the entire church. . . . It is the one and only Holy Spirit who distributes these gifts. He alone decides which gift each person should have. 1 Corinthians 12:7, 11

Every good and perfect gift is from above, coming down from the Father of the heavenly lights, who does not change like shifting shadows. James 1:17 NIV

The Spirit and the bride say, "Come!" And let him who hears say, "Come!" Whoever is thirsty, let him come; and whoever wishes, let him take the free gift of the water of life. Revelation 22:17 NIV

25

Escape to Slavery

Scripture Passage: Philemon

So What? Jesus can set you free!

For Parents: [Anything in brackets]

What is a slave? What's the difference between a worker and a slave? Would you like to be a slave? Why would you want that? Why would you not want to be one? Do you sometimes feel like a slave when you have to do your chores?

Onesimus was a slave in the Roman Empire. In some countries there are still slaves today. Being a slave means you are someone else's property. Owning a slave is like owning a bike. You can buy it and sell it. You can take good care of it or you can abuse it. Slaves get no money for what they do. A master owns his or her slave in the same way that you own your toys and clothes. If I were your slave, you would own me. You could buy me and sell me. You could give me away and separate me from my family.

In Rome, some slaves had masters that treated them nicely. Other slaves were beaten and treated cruelly [like the Jewish people in Egypt]. A rich man and his wife owned Onesimus; their names were Philemon and Apphia. As far as we know, they treated him well, but Onesimus hated slavery. He hated the fact that they could buy and sell him like a box of Legos. He decided to escape!

If you were a slave, would you try to run away? Do you know what would happen if you were caught?

If you were a slave who ran away, and the authorities found you, it was bad news. It was very, very bad news. The owner could do whatever he wanted with you. Often owners would have the slaves crucified (just as Jesus was). Other owners would actually work their slaves to death; they would make them work and work with very little sleep or food until they died. Most slaves didn't run away because they were afraid someone would catch them.

Onesimus was afraid someone might catch him too, but he ran away anyway. It probably happened something like this . . .

While working in Philemon's house, Onesimus stole some things he could sell for money, probably some jewelry belonging to Apphia and other small things he could pack easily. Then, late at night, when everyone was asleep, he snuck out of the big house and onto the street. He ran and hid all night, hoping to find someone with whom he could hitch a ride. He went as fast as he could toward the biggest known city in the world: Rome. Even though he'd have to travel a thousand miles on dangerous roads and ships, he thought he would be safe in Rome. [Look at a map in the back of the Bible. He is leaving the area of Ephesus. What roads might he take? How long would it take?] There he could hide and hopefully never be found. So he snuck, and he hid, and he lied about who he was, and he found a ride, and he got on a ship, and he hid some more, and he lied again, and he got another ride, and finally he arrived in Rome.

In Rome, he still felt like a slave. He had to lie about who he was. He had to sneak around. He was no longer a slave to Philemon, but he was still a slave. He knew he wasn't free.

What's the difference between a prisoner and a slave? Which one has the most freedom?

When Onesimus was in Rome, he heard somebody preaching. The person preaching was in chains; he was a prisoner to Rome. He had chains on his wrists and ankles [kind of like handcuffs] to make sure he didn't run away. There was a Roman guard with him all the time, wherever he went. But this guy was preaching about being free. And he said things like, "So Christ has really set us free. Now make sure that you stay free, and don't get tied up again in slavery to the law. . . . You have died with Christ, and he has set you free from the evil powers of this world" (Gal. 5:1; Col. 2:20). Even though Paul was under house arrest, even though he was a prisoner in Rome, his spirit felt free. Here was a person in chains who felt free. And there was Onesimus, with no chains, who felt like a slave.

Paul was the preacher. Onesimus met Paul and asked him, "Paul, tell me something. How can you feel free? There's a guard right next to you. He's with you all the time. There are shackles on your hands and feet. You're a prisoner of Rome. They can chop your head off tomorrow if they want to. How can you feel free?"

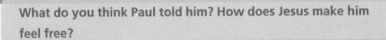

What do you think Paul told him? How does Jesus make him feel free?

Paul must have explained to Onesimus, "In this new life, it doesn't matter if you are a Jew or a Gentile, circumcised or uncircumcised, barbaric, uncivilized, slave, or free. Christ is all that matters. . . . He gave his life to free us from every kind of sin, to cleanse us, and to make us his very own people, totally committed to doing what is right" (Col. 3:11; Titus 2:14). In other words I'm a slave to Jesus because I want to be. He died for me, and I love him. That makes me free from anyone else. I'll do anything and everything Jesus asks me to do. That makes me free. I feel free inside because my spirit is free. I serve Jesus and no one else.

When Onesimus heard that, he said, "You know what? I have been serving myself all my life. I'm a slave to my desires. I want to do things for me. I thought if I didn't have to serve my master anymore, I could live for myself and be happy. I stole some things and I rode the boat all the way over here and I spent the money on myself, but I still don't feel free."

Paul explained, "That's why faith is the key! God's promise is given to us as a free gift" (Rom. 4:16). Before you can feel free, you have to get rid of your sin. There's only one way to get rid of sin. That's through Jesus. If you believe in Jesus, he'll set you free. He'll wash your sin away and keep you from having to be a slave to your old desires.

Onesimus gave his life to Jesus. He was still a slave, but he was free! Later he told Paul his story. "You know what?" he probably asked. "I was a slave for years, and I ran away. My master wasn't a bad sort of person, not for a slave master anyway. This may sound crazy, Paul, but I'm starting to feel guilty about running away. I stole from Philemon, and I ran 1,000 miles away. I still kind of feel guilty about that, even though Jesus set me free from everything I did wrong."

A shocked Paul answered, "Wow, you won't believe this, but I think I know this guy Philemon! There's a church that meets in his house, right?"

"Yeah, there is. I used to have to set up chairs for it and clean up when it was over. They could leave a real mess some Sundays."

"Onesimus, I believe you need to go back. Your guilt is from the Holy Spirit. Jesus would want you to go back to Philemon and tell him you're sorry you ran away."

"What? No way; I can't do that!"

"There is a way. Jesus can give you the courage to obey."

Would you go back? Would you be scared? What could Philemon do to you if you were his runaway slave?

The Book of Philemon is a letter Paul wrote to his friend, Philemon. Paul asked Philemon to be kind to Onesimus and to accept him back, not as a slave, but as a fellow believer in Jesus. Onesimus carried the letter back with him. He traveled back 1,000 miles to where he was a slave. He escaped back to slavery.

Do you know what happened when Onesimus went back to Philemon with the letter? Neither do I! The Bible doesn't say. Philemon could have made Onesimus a slave again or set him free. We don't know. It really doesn't matter. What does matter is what we do know. We know that Jesus set Onesimus free. Slave, prisoner, or free man, Onesimus would never be a slave to his desires again. Anyone Jesus sets free is free indeed!

Remember: You've Got His Word on It

I cried out to the LORD in my suffering, and he heard me. He set me free from all my fears. Psalm 34:6

We escaped like a bird from a hunter's trap. The trap is broken, and we are free! Psalm 124:7

I have swept away your sins like the morning mists. I have scattered your offenses like the clouds. Oh, return to me, for I have paid the price to set you free. . . . Is anyone thirsty? Come and drink—even if you have no money! Come, take your choice of wine or milk—it's all free! Isaiah 44:22; 55:1

But for you who fear my name, the Sun of Righteousness will rise with healing in his wings. And you will go free, leaping with joy like calves let out to pasture. Malachi 4:2

So if the Son sets you free, you will indeed be free. John 8:36

He will keep you strong right up to the end, and he will keep you free from all blame on the great day when our Lord Jesus Christ returns. 1 Corinthians 1:8

He has set you free from the evil powers of this world. Colossians 2:20

26

One Big City

Scripture Passage: Revelation 21

So What? One day you can live in the crystal city!

For Parents: [Anything in brackets—If you can find an atlas of the United States and Canada for this story, it will help to visualize the size of the crystal city.]

> Would you like to see the future? How far in the future would you like to see? Would you like to see your life five years from now? Would you like to look ahead ten years? What might it look like 1,000 years from now?

God allowed the apostle John to see the future. John lived 2,000 years ago, and God took him so far into the future that what John saw hasn't even happened yet! In fact, some things John saw are still over 1,000 years ahead of today! Would you like to know what will happen in a thousand years? Good, because John wrote down what he saw!

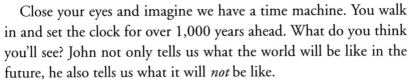

If you could make the perfect world, what would not be in it?

Close your eyes and imagine we have a time machine. You walk in and set the clock for over 1,000 years ahead. What do you think you'll see? John not only tells us what the world will be like in the future, he also tells us what it will *not* be like.

John tells us that 1,000+ years from now, we will be living on a new earth. The earth we know will be gone, and God will make a new one. Some things we have here will be missing there. Here are some things that will be missing:

- Tears—There will be no more crying, ever! If we will never cry again, what else might be missing?
- Death—No one will ever die again. There will be no more dead friends, pets, or tortoises. There will be no more funerals. If there is no more death, what else might be missing?
- Sadness—If we are never sad again, what will life be like?
- Pain—If there is no more pain, what else might be missing?
- Sin—All who desire to practice sin, who refuse to believe in Jesus, will be gone 1,000+ years from now.
- Church and temple buildings—There will be no need for church buildings because Jesus will be living with us!

We call the new earth heaven.

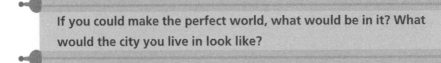

If you could make the perfect world, what would be in it? What would the city you live in look like?

Now we know what the new earth 1,000+ years from now doesn't have. But John also tells us what it does have. This new earth, heaven, has one big, beautiful city. The city John saw is where all Christians and angels will live. Here are some things we know about the city:

It will be built out of some kind of gold that is bright and clear like crystal.

It will have beautiful walls around it that are over two hundred feet thick. That's probably about as thick as ten of your houses stacked on top of each other!

It will be made with all kinds of huge, beautiful stones set into bright clear gold.

It will have God instead of the sun to give it light.

It will be called "The New Jerusalem."

It will have Jesus instead of a church building as a place of worship.

It will have only those who believe in Jesus living in it.

It will be *one big city!*

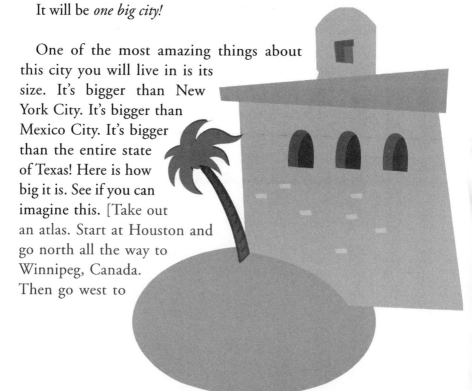

One of the most amazing things about this city you will live in is its size. It's bigger than New York City. It's bigger than Mexico City. It's bigger than the entire state of Texas! Here is how big it is. See if you can imagine this. [Take out an atlas. Start at Houston and go north all the way to Winnipeg, Canada. Then go west to

Vancouver Island and go south to San Diego. Now go back east to Houston.] All of this area, over one-half the size of the United States, is the size of the city Jesus is preparing for you! But, that is not the entire size of the city. It's not even half of it!

This city you will be living in is fifteen hundred miles long (from Houston to Winnipeg, Vancouver Island to San Diego). And it's fifteen hundred miles wide (from Houston to San Diego, Vancouver Island to Winnipeg). What shape does that make the city? Right, it's a square. But that's not all; that's only a little part of the city! It's also fifteen hundred miles high! Now what shape is it? [A cube or a pyramid.] That means this crystal city will go up higher than planes fly. It will even be higher than the satellites that orbit our planet. That makes this city bigger than 1,000 states of the United States on top of each other! This is one big city! How many stairs do you think it would take to get to the top? I sure hope it has good elevators! Maybe God will make us so we can fly then. [The city John calls "The New Jerusalem" is about fifteen hundred miles square—and high. Some believe that this just means that it is big, that the measurements are symbolic. That may be your belief and the belief you want to pass on to your children. For some reason, though, God had the angel measure the entire city, state that it was being measured in human measurements, give those measurements to John, and have John write them down. It's my assumption God did that because those measurements are real and accurate.]

> What has Jesus done for you? What is sin? Do you still sin? Do you still want to sin?

One-thousand-plus years from now there will be no more crying, pain, or death because there will be no more sin. Sin is doing anything against God. Since God is perfect, good, and right, sin is leaving his path and doing things that are imperfect, bad, and wrong. There won't be any sin allowed in the crystal city. That's what makes this big city a wonderful place to live in.

The problem is—all of us have sinned, so how can we get into the city? Jesus came and died for us to take our sins away. If we believe in him, he will remove our sins so we can live with him forever in the crystal city. Here's how it works.

The moment we believe in Jesus and ask him to wash our sins away, he rescues us from the penalty of sin. Jesus paid the price for our sins, and they're gone! After we believe in Jesus, we still want to sin. It is a bad habit of ours. But Jesus has also saved us from the power of our sinful habits. We don't have to sin anymore. We can choose to sin, but we can also choose not to sin.

The problem is, here on earth sin is still all around us. Even if you never sin again, the effects of sin will get to you. You will still feel pain and sorrow. People will still pick on you and be mean to you. But someday we'll die, or Jesus will come for us, and we'll be saved from the presence of sin. Sin will be gone forever. There will be a new earth where we will live in one big city with Jesus!

Truth is, until Jesus comes, you'll still choose to sin sometimes. Sin can be fun for a short time. That's partly why you do it. Sin is a habit. If someone yells at you, do you want to respond sweetly? Nah, you probably want to yell right back—only louder! The weakness to give in to sin will be gone in our new city called heaven.

Heaven won't be boring, painful, or dull. It will be great—greater than anything you can imagine. Imagine a perfect day. It'll be better than that!

Remember: You've Got His Word on It

I saw a new heaven and a new earth, because the first heaven and earth had disappeared, and the sea was gone. Then I saw the holy city, New Jerusalem, coming down from God out of heaven, dressed like a bride ready for her husband. I heard a loud voice from the throne say, "God lives with humans! God will make his home with them, and they will be his people. God himself will be with them and be their God. He will wipe every tear from their eyes. There won't be any more death. There won't be any grief, crying, or pain, because the first things have disappeared."

The one sitting on the throne said, "I am making everything new." He said, "Write this: These words are faithful and true." He said to me, "It has happened! I am the A and the Z, the beginning and the end. I will give a drink from the fountain filled with the water of life to anyone who is thirsty. It won't cost anything. Everyone who wins the victory will inherit these things. I will be their God, and they will be my children." Revelation 21:1–7 (GOD'S WORD)

Books That Helped

Bible Knowledge Commentary: OT underlying source materials. Wheaton, Ill.: Victor Books, Scripture Press Publishers, 1985. NavPress Software, 1997.

Bible Knowledge Commentary: NT underlying source materials. Wheaton, Ill.: Victor Books, Scripture Press Publishers, 1983. NavPress Software, 1997.

Egermeier, Elsie E. *Egermeier's Bible Story Book.* Anderson, Ind.: Warner Press, 1955.

Enhanced Nave's Topics. NavPress Software, 1994.

iExalt Bible Software. iExalt, Inc., 1987–2000. All rights reserved.

International Standard Bible Encyclopaedia. NavPress Software, 1998.

JFB Commentary. iExalt, Inc., 2000.

Keener, Craig S. *The IVP Bible Background Commentary: New Testament.* Downers Grove, Ill.: InterVarsity Press, 1993. NavPress Software, 1997.

Matthew Henry's Commentary. NavPress Software, 1996.

McDowell, Josh. *The New Evidence That Demands a Verdict.* Nashville: Thomas Nelson, 1999.

NAS Hebrew-Aramaic and Greek Dictionaries. Lockman Foundation, 1981, 1998. iExalt, Inc., 2000.

Strong's Greek and Hebrew Dictionary. NavPress Software, 1990–93.

Teacher's Commentary. Wheaton, Ill.: Victor, Scripture Press Publishers, 1983. NavPress Software, 1997.

The New Greek-English Interlinear New Testament. Wheaton, Ill. Tyndale, 1990.

The New Unger's Bible Dictionary. Chicago, Ill.: Moody, 1988. NavPress Software, 1997.

Theological Workbook of the Old Testament. Chicago, Ill.: The Moody Bible Institute, 1980. iExalt, Inc., 1999.

Walton, John H., and Victor H. Matthews. *The IVP Bible Background Commentary: Genesis-Deuteronomy.* Downers Grove, Ill.: InterVarsity Press, 1998. NavPress Software, 1997.

Acknowledgments

The year was 1976, and I was scared to death. It was staff training week at Camp Peniel. David Whitelock, program director, was teaching us how to tell Bible stories to campers who would be there in less than a week. Bible stories bored me; how could I tell boring stories to a cabin full of restless campers? David, rather than telling us how to tell stories, told us a story—"The Loud Army That Wasn't," from 2 Kings 6:24–7:20. I had read the story before (Bible College made us read the entire Bible), but I sure didn't remember it. "Aha," I decided. "I'll find a bunch of unknown Bible stories to keep my campers listening!" I did, and they did. Thank you, David!

Eleven years later, I woke up to find myself the proud father of two young girls (Megan and Amanda aren't twins, but they were just one diaper size apart), the oldest of which needed a devotion time. "Self," I said, "what do I do now? I know—Peniel Bible stories!" Thus began the fun task of retelling those exciting Bible stories to my own children. Thanks Megan and Amanda!

A few years ago, I was reading a devotional book to my young boys, Micah and Caleb. Telling a story is work, you see, reading them is much simpler. Micah said to me, "Don't bother to read to us tonight, Dad; we already know all the stories." "You know all the stories in the Bible?" "Sure, we've heard them all a dozen times!" I then went through every remaining story in the devotional book I was using. Micah was right; he and his little brother Caleb knew every story. Bummer. "Okay, wise ones, see if you know this story!" I found Micah's Bible and turned to 2 Kings 6:24–7:20. Thank you Micah and Caleb!

The need to get the Bible into our children is of infinite value for the rest of their lives. These stories worked for my kids, so I thought they might work for others. Deanna got me in touch with her agent. Les got me in touch with a dozen book companies. They weren't as excited as my children and I were. I finally decided to start writing the stories, so that sometime (Megan and Amanda are allowed to date when they are 30) they may even be read to my grandkids. I would spiral bind them at the office store; it shouldn't cost too much. Then Jeanette at Baker Books called. She shared our excitement! Les and Baker Books wanted to know if the book contract "was acceptable." "Acceptable? I would have paid *you* to print them!" Thank you, Deanna, Les, and Jeanette!

I tried to write this book but realized that I can't think without my mouth open. So I retold the stories to Micah and Caleb with the cassette recorder going. My wife, JoLynn, kindly typed them all into the computer, run-on sentences, Caleb interruptions, and all. From there I made the text into readable stories. I sent those to my sister Janice Jones, a schoolteacher and author of poems and short stories. After fixing the grammar and removing a few hundred "that's" she sent them back to me. From there JoLynn gave the stories another edit. Then I edited them again and finally they went off to Baker Books, who let us know why we aren't professional editors! At any rate, it was a fun family project. Thank you, JoLynn, Janice, and our wonderful, unpredictable God for terrific true stories!

Index

Dan Cooley, senior pastor of Elim Chapel in Winnipeg, Canada, started telling bizarre Bible stories as a teen to young campers twenty-five years ago at Camp Peniel in Marble Falls, Texas. Dan's four children grew up listening to these same stories, and his desire to pass them to his grandchildren (okay—there aren't any yet, but one must think ahead . . . yes, even waaay ahead) brought them into print for parents, grandparents, and Sunday school teachers—anyone who wants to get kids into the Bible and the Bible into kids!

The first bizarre Bible story Dan heard was "The Loud Army that Wasn't" during staff training at Camp Peniel in 1976. He was a camp counselor/director there for eight years and a children's and youth pastor for thirteen additional years. He has a BA in theology from Dallas Bible College and an MA in ministry from Moody Graduate School.

He and his family love rappelling, mountain-bike riding, all things about *The Princess Bride* and VeggieTales, hot weather, and hotter Mexican food—and chocolate. The Cooleys live in the central plains of Canada, where they can often be found sitting around the fireplace, eating chips and salsa while looking up more bizarre Bible stories in Scripture.

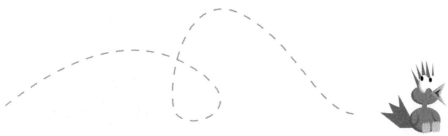

Garry Colby, a professional illustrator in Florida, works on children's books, magazine features, and advertising for everyone from McDonald's, Kellogg and Post Cereal, to Sears, Hasbro, and Lego—just not all in the same day. He's taught art at the Center for Creative Studies Art College in Detroit and attended Wayne State University. His art has been recognized in New York Illustration Show, New York Art Directors Club, and *Print* magazine; he's been awarded gold and silver medals in Caddy Club's annual show and Scarab Club's annual competition. His perfect day would start with windsurfing on the Intercoastal, shopping in Boca, and strolling the Art Deco District on South Beach.

This book has been read by

_____